DOMINOES

Sherlock Holmes: The Sign of Four

LEVEL THREE   1000 HEADWORDS

OXFORD

UNIVERSITY PRESS

Great Clarendon Street, Oxford OX2 6DP

Oxford University Press is a department of the University of Oxford.
It furthers the University's objective of excellence in research, scholarship,
and education by publishing worldwide in

Oxford New York

Auckland Cape Town Dar es Salaam Hong Kong Karachi
Kuala Lumpur Madrid Melbourne Mexico City Nairobi
New Delhi Shanghai Taipei Toronto

With offices in

Argentina Austria Brazil Chile Czech Republic France Greece
Guatemala Hungary Italy Japan Poland Portugal Singapore
South Korea Switzerland Thailand Turkey Ukraine Vietnam

OXFORD and OXFORD ENGLISH are registered trade marks of
Oxford University Press in the UK and in certain other countries

ISBN: 978 0 19 424823 5 BOOK
ISBN: 978 0 19 463982 8 BOOK AND AUDIO PACK

No unauthorized photocopying

Printed in China

This book is printed on paper from certified and well-managed sources.

ACKNOWLEDGEMENTS

Illustrations by: Nick Hardcastle (main story), Susan Scott (cover).

The publisher would like to thank the following for permission to reproduce photographs: Alamy
Images ppiv (Red Fort, Pradesh, India/SCPhotos), 6 (Lyceum Theatre/Hoberman Collection
UK), 56 (Baker Street sign/PSL Images), 57 (Houses of Parliament/Robert Harding Picture
Library Ltd), 76 (Galapagos/David Hosking), 76 (Tasmania/Bill Bachman); Corbis pp20
(Colonial House, India/Hans Georg Roth), 49 (East End children/Hulton-Deutsch Collection),
74 (Ko Hong Island/Jose Fuste Raga), 76 (Robben Island/Hoberman Collection); Getty Images
p12 (House of Parliament/Sylvester Adams/Taxi); Mary Evans Picture Library pp29 (Upper
Norwood, postcard 1900c), 37 (Police launch/Thames Police Museum), 48 (Andaman Islands
1890's); Oxford University Press pp36 (Persian carpet/Sdbphoto carpets), 63 (crocodile/John
Kasawa); Shutterstock p75 (Devil's island in French Guiana/Stephanie Rousseau).

DOMINOES

Series Editors: Bill Bowler and Sue Parminter

Sherlock Holmes: The Sign of Four

Sir Arthur Conan Doyle

Text adaptation by Jeremy Page

Illustrated by Nick Hardcastle

Sir Arthur Conan Doyle (1859–1930), born in Edinburgh, Scotland, is best known as the creator of Sherlock Holmes. He started writing after working as a doctor and soon became one of the world's best-known authors. *Sherlock Holmes: The Blue Diamond*, *The Emerald Crown* and *The Norwood Mystery* are also available as Dominoes. His adventure story *The Lost World* is also a Domino title.

OXFORD
UNIVERSITY PRESS

BEFORE READING

1 Match the sentences with the pictures of people from *The Sign of Four*.

Sherlock Holmes

Dr Watson

Miss Morstan

Thaddeus Sholto

Major Sholto

Mordecai Smith

Jonathan Small

Tonga

a She's a thoughtful young woman.

b He was born on an island near India.

c He was an officer in the British army.

d He studied medicine at university.

e He's a clever and famous detective.

f He's a strange young man.

g He works on the River Thames.

h He's had a hard life and been to prison.

2 This is the fort at Agra, in India. Which sentences about it are true, do you think? Tick the boxes.

a It was a prison for Shah Jehan, the man who built the Taj Mahal. ☐

b The Indians fought against the British here in 1857. ☐

c The Egyptian singer Hisham Abbas made a music video here in 2000. ☐

Chapter one

Miss Mary Morstan

In the summer of 1888 I was living with my good friend Sherlock Holmes, the famous detective, in Baker Street. He was so highly intelligent that he never failed to surprise me.

One morning in July he turned to me lazily and said: 'Watson, if I am not wrong, you have been to the post office in Wigmore Street to send a **telegram**.'

He was, of course, quite right, but I had no idea how he could know this. I had told no one.

'Very good, Holmes,' I replied. 'Did you follow me when I went out?'

'No, Watson,' Holmes smiled.

'Then perhaps you will explain,' I said, a little **impatiently**.

'**Elementary**, Watson,' my friend replied. 'There's a little reddish **mud** on your shoe. Outside the post office in Wigmore Street, men are working on the road. I saw them yesterday. The ground there is red, and it's impossible to enter the post office without stepping in it.'

'As you say, Holmes, elementary,' I said. 'And the telegram?'

'Because we were here together all morning, I knew that you hadn't written a letter. There are stamps and postcards on your desk, so why did you go to the post office and not a post box? To send a telegram, of course!'

telegram a very short letter that you send very quickly

impatiently not happily, because you are unable to wait for someting

elementary very easy

mud very wet ground

At that moment there was a knock on the door and our **housekeeper**, Mrs Hudson, entered.

'There's a young lady to see you,' she informed us. 'Miss Mary Morstan.'

'Mary Morstan,' Holmes repeated. 'I don't recognize the name. Please ask her to come in, Mrs Hudson.'

He turned to me.

'Don't go, Doctor. Please stay and listen to the lady's story.'

I was happy to do as he said. When Miss Morstan came into the room, she seemed calm, but it was clear that she didn't want to **waste** any time. She was a young woman, small, with fair hair. Her clothes showed good taste, but they weren't expensive. She had a pleasant face and beautiful blue eyes. She looked serious and intelligent, but not, I thought, rich. Holmes invited her to sit down and, as she took her seat, for the first time she seemed worried. Mrs Hudson left us, and our visitor began her story.

'Mr Holmes,' she said, 'I find myself in a very strange **situation.** I don't understand it at all.'

My friend Sherlock Holmes looked very interested.

'Please tell us everything,' he said.

'My father was an officer in the army,' she continued. 'He was sent to India, where I was born. Two years later, my mother died and I was sent home to Scotland. I lived in a small hotel in Edinburgh until I was seventeen. In 1878 my father returned from India. He sent me a telegram from London asking me to travel south to meet him. He wrote that he was looking forward to seeing me. I took the train to London, then drove to his hotel, but he wasn't there. They told me that **Captain** Morstan had gone out the night before and had not returned. I waited all day, but there was no news of him so I went to the police. The next day I put an **advertisement** in all the newspapers, but there was still no news. And since then I have heard nothing of my father.'

housekeeper a woman who looks after a rich person's house

waste to use badly

situation when things are happening around you and you feel in the middle of them

captain the leader of a group of soldiers

advertisement you pay to put this in a newspaper

'What was the date of his disappearance?' asked Holmes.

'The 3rd of December 1878,' she replied. 'Ten years ago.'

'And his luggage?' Holmes continued.

'It stayed at his hotel. I searched his suitcases but found only clothes and books and some **souvenirs** from the Andaman Islands in the Bay of Bengal. My father worked as an officer at the British prison there for some years before he **retired**.'

Holmes thought for a moment.

'Did your father have any friends in London?' he asked.

'Only one: **Major** Sholto, who was an officer with my father in India. He had retired six months before my father and was living in Norwood. I wrote to him, but he wrote back to say that he didn't even know my father was in England.'

'Very strange,' said Holmes.

souvenir a thing that you buy to remind you of a place

retire to stop working when you are old

major an officer in the army

'There is more,' Miss Morstan went on. 'Six years ago I saw an advertisement in *The Times*. It asked for my address and informed me that there was good news. There was no name or address. At that time I had just started working for Mrs Forrester's family, as a **governess.** I replied to the advertisement, and that same day I **received** a small box in the post. In it, I found a very large **pearl**. There was no message. Since then, every year on the same day I have received a pearl in the post. They are worth a lot of money, Mr Holmes. And they're also very beautiful.'

As she spoke, she took a flat box from her bag, opened it and showed us six beautiful pearls.

'I find your story strangely exciting,' said Holmes. 'Do you have anything else to tell us, Miss Morstan?'

'One more thing,' she replied. 'This morning I received this letter. Perhaps you would like to read it.'

'Yes,' said Holmes. 'And can I see the **envelope**, please?' He studied the envelope carefully. 'This was posted in London, on 7 July – yesterday. There's a man's **fingerprint** on the envelope, probably the postman's. The paper and envelope are expensive, but there's no address, of course.'

He then went on to read the letter aloud: ' "Come to the Lyceum Theatre this evening at seven o'clock and wait outside the front door. You can bring two friends, but you must not bring the police. I have good news for you. Your unknown friend." What a mystery! So what's your plan, Miss Morstan?'

'I don't know,' she replied. 'That's why I have come to you, Mr Holmes. Please tell me what I should do.'

governess a woman who lives with and teaches children in their home

receive to get something that somebody sends to you

pearl a small, round, expensive stone that is found in a shellfish

envelope a paper cover that you put a letter in

fingerprint a mark that is made by the lines on the end of your finger

'You must go to the Lyceum this evening,' said Holmes. 'Dr Watson and I will come with you, won't we, Watson?'

'Of course,' I answered. 'If you think that could be helpful.'

'Thank you both so much,' said Miss Morstan. 'You're very kind. My life in Norwood is quiet and I have no friends. Shall I come here at six o'clock this evening?'

'Yes,' Holmes replied. 'But I have one more question for you, Miss Morstan. Is the writing in the letter the same as the writing of the addresses on the pearl boxes?'

'Yes,' said Miss Morstan, taking some papers from her bag.

'Excellent!' cried Holmes. 'Let me see.'

The great detective looked carefully at the writing in the letter and the addresses. He seemed very pleased.

'They were written by the same hand,' he informed us.

'Is it possible that this is your father's writing?' he asked.

'No. His writing was quite different,' she told us.

'That answer doesn't surprise me,' said Holmes. 'We'll see you at six. Please leave the papers here. Goodbye, Miss Morstan.'

The young lady stood up to leave, and smiled.

'Goodbye, Mr Holmes. Goodbye, Dr Watson.'

'Until this evening,' I said, looking into her blue eyes.

I heard her go down the stairs and out into Baker Street. From the window I watched her walk away down the street.

'A very fine woman, Holmes,' I said.

'Really?' my friend replied lazily. 'I didn't notice. Now, what do you think of this writing?'

'A businessman's, perhaps,' I answered.

'I don't think so, Watson,' he replied. 'The writer sometimes finds it difficult to decide what to do.'

'I'm going out,' he informed me, standing up. 'I need to think some more. I'll be back in an hour.'

My friend left me alone in the room. Everywhere I looked, I saw the face of our visitor, Miss Mary Morstan. I waited impatiently for six o'clock and her return.

READING CHECK

Tick the boxes to complete the sentences.

a The story begins . . .

   1 ☐ at the post office in Wigmore Street.

   2 ☐ outside the post office in Wigmore Street.

   3 ☑ in Holmes's and Watson's rooms in Baker Street.

b To Dr Watson Miss Morstan seems . . .

   1 ☐ clever and rich, with good taste.

   2 ☐ small, young and expensively dressed.

   3 ☐ serious and good-looking, but not rich.

c Captain Morstan . . .

   1 ☐ recently travelled from India to Edinburgh.

   2 ☐ is staying in a hotel in London.

   3 ☐ travelled from India to London ten years earlier.

d Six years earlier, Miss Morstan . . .

   1 ☐ sent an advertisement to *The Times*.

   2 ☐ answered an advertisement in *The Times*.

   3 ☐ bought a very large pearl.

e Since then, every year on the same day, . . .

   1 ☐ a pearl arrives for Miss Morstan in the post.

   2 ☐ Miss Morstan gets a letter from her father.

   3 ☐ Miss Morstan puts a new advertisement in *The Times*.

f On the morning of the day that Miss Morstan visits Sherlock Holmes . . .

   1 ☐ six pearls arrived for her.

   2 ☐ she got a letter inviting her to a meeting at the Lyceum theatre.

   3 ☐ a letter arrived for her from the Lyceum theatre.

g Sherlock Holmes agrees . . .

   1 ☐ to send Dr Watson to the Lyceum that evening.

   2 ☐ to meet Miss Morstan at the Lyceum that evening.

   3 ☐ to go to the Lyceum with Miss Morstan and Dr Watson that evening.

WORD WORK

Correct the words in these sentences. They all come from Chapter 1.

a It was raining, and he got **much** on his shoes when he walked across the park. .mud..

b Watson goes to the post office to send a **telegraph**. ....

c Don't **taste** that paper. Write on the back of it too! ....

d My father used to be a music teacher, but he **required** last year and doesn't work now. ....

e Miss Morstan works as a **governor** for the Forrester family. ....

f Holmes finds a **footprint** on the envelope. ....

g Have you **deceived** any news from your daughter in Thailand? ....

h I find myself in a difficult **sensation** and don't know what to do. ....

i He was late, and Jane was waiting for him very **importantly** outside the cinema when he arrived. ....

j At the end of our holiday in Turkey we brought some lovely **engineers** from a little shop in Istanbul. ....

GUESS WHAT

Match the first and second parts of these sentences to find out what happens in the next chapter.

a Holmes tells Watson

b Miss Morstan arrives

c Miss Morstan shows Holmes

d Holmes studies Captain Morstan's paper

e Holmes, Watson and Miss Morstan

f The cab takes them

1 in Baker Street in a cab.

2 are driven through the streets of London.

3 everything that he has found out about Major Sholto.

4 to south London.

5 with great interest.

6 a strange paper which she found in her father's desk.

A Strange Paper

It was half past five when Holmes returned to our rooms. He seemed bright and excited.

'Watson,' he said, 'everything is clear to me now.'

'Really?' I asked. I was very surprised.

Holmes lit a cigarette and sat down.

'I've discovered a very interesting fact,' he went on.

'So the mystery is **solved**,' I said.

Holmes looked at me with his bright, clear eyes.

'No, Watson,' he replied, 'but I am beginning to understand.'

'What have you discovered?' I asked.

'I read in the Times of 29 April 1882 that Major Sholto, an army officer, died the day before in Norwood, south London.'

'But why is that important, Holmes,' I asked.

Holmes looked at me kindly.

'Let me explain,' he replied. 'Captain Morstan disappears in London. He knows only one person here, Major Sholto, so we must suppose he visited Major Sholto. But the Major says he never knew Captain Morstan was in England. Four years later he dies. A few days after that, Morstan's daughter receives a valuable present. There is good news at last – but of what? Of her father, Watson! And why did Miss Morstan start to receive presents so soon after Sholto's death?'

'I'm sorry, Holmes,' I replied, 'I have no idea.'

'Because the Major's heir knows something about this mystery and wants to tell Miss Morstan everything that he knows. Can there be another explanation, Watson?'

He finished his cigarette while I thought about his words.

'I'm sure you're right, Holmes,' I said at last. 'But why did the letter come this year, not six years ago? And what is this news of Miss Morstan's father? After six years without seeing his daughter he can't possibly be alive.'

solve to find the answer to a mystery

'True,' Holmes agreed, 'but we'll learn more tonight. And here is Miss Morstan now in a **cab**. Are you ready?'

We stood up, and went down the stairs and out into Baker Street. I noticed that Holmes brought his **revolver** with him. It was clear he thought that we might be in danger.

In the cab we found Miss Morstan, dressed in black. She was calm, but her face was white. She seemed happy to answer the questions that Holmes asked her on our journey.

'Were your father and Major Sholto close friends?'

'Very close,' she replied. 'Father wrote about the Major in every letter he sent me. They worked together as officers in the Andaman Islands for some time, you see.'

Holmes looked thoughtful.

'Do you have any of your father's letters with you?' he asked.

'No, but I have a very strange paper, which I found in my father's desk. It probably isn't important.'

Miss Morstan took the paper from her bag and gave it to Holmes, who looked at it very carefully.

cab a taxi
revolver a gun

'It was made in India,' he told us, 'and it seems to be a plan of a very big house with several halls and **passages** and a large number of rooms. There's a red **cross**, which perhaps shows where something important is, and four black crosses in a line with the words, 'The **Sign** of Four' – Jonathan Small, Mahomet Singh, Abdullah Khan, Dost Akbar. No, I don't understand the importance of this paper, but I'm sure it *is* important. Keep it safe, Miss Morstan, it may be useful to us.'

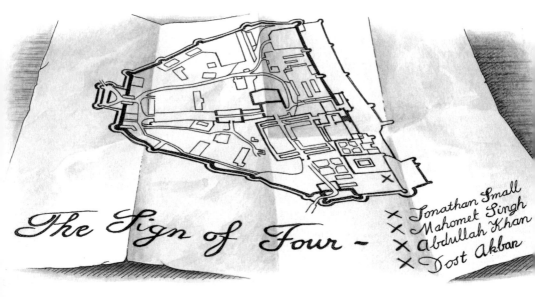

The Sign of Four – × Jonathan Small × Mahomet Singh × Abdullah Khan × Dost Akbar

As we drove to the Lyceum, Miss Morstan and I spoke quietly together, but Holmes said nothing more. He was thinking.

It was a strangely cold evening, and the sky was grey and full of clouds. There was thick **fog** in the streets of London and it was difficult to see the street **lamps** as we drove along. Everything seemed unreal in their strange, yellow light. The grey, wet evening made me feel sad. Miss Morstan, too, looked serious and lost in thought.

When we arrived at the theatre, the street was full of people. I paid our driver, and we walked to the main door of the theatre. It was exactly seven o'clock.

Immediately a small, dark man came towards us, and asked, 'Are you the **gentlemen** who have come with Miss Morstan?'

'I am Miss Morstan, and these are my friends,' she replied.

The man studied her carefully.

'I'm sorry, Miss Morstan,' he said, 'but I have to ask you if these gentlemen are police officers.'

'I promise you they aren't,' Miss Morstan answered him.

'Then will you please follow me?' he said.

We followed him to a cab and got inside. He climbed into the driver's seat and **whipped** the horse, and soon we were travelling quickly through the foggy streets. We had, of course, no idea where we were going or what we would find there. I told Miss Morstan stories of my time in Afghanistan, but I was so excited that I soon realized she was finding it difficult to follow me.

Holmes looked out of the window and from time to time he told us where we were at that moment on our long journey.

'We're crossing the Thames now,' he said as we drove over Vauxhall Bridge.

I looked out and saw the silent water of the river below us through the fog. Our cab moved quickly on and soon we were in one of the poorest parts of south London. There were streets of tall, grey houses with brightly lit pubs on every corner. Finally we stopped outside the third house in an **ugly** street of new buildings. The other houses were all in darkness, but in this house there was a light at the kitchen window. Our driver got down from his seat and opened the door of the cab. We followed him to the door of the house. He knocked loudly and the door was immediately opened. An Indian **servant** stood in front of us.

'Mr Sholto is waiting for you,' he said.

Suddenly we heard a strange, high voice from inside the house.

'Bring them to me!' it said. 'Bring them to me now!'

gentleman a man from a good family, usually rich

whip to hit with a special long thin stick

ugly not beautiful

servant a person who works for someone rich

READING CHECK

Are these sentences true or false? Tick the boxes.

		True	False
a	Miss Morstan returns to Baker Street before Holmes.	☐	☑
b	Holmes reads about Captain Morstan's death in an old newspaper.	☐	☐
c	Holmes knows for sure that Captain Morstan visited Major Sholto in London before he died.	☐	☐
d	When Holmes and Watson leave their rooms in Baker Street, Holmes takes his gun with him.	☐	☐
e	Miss Morstan explains that her father and Sholto worked together in the Andaman Islands.	☐	☐
f	Holmes understands why the plan of the big house is so important.	☐	☐
g	They meet a dark man at the Lyceum theatre who takes them to a cab.	☐	☐
h	The cab takes them to a very poor part of south London.	☐	☐

WORD WORK

1 Find words from Chapter 2 in the fog.

servantsolveuglygentlemanwhipsrevolverlampscrossespassagessign

2 Complete these sentences with words from Activity 1.

a Can Sherlock Holmes solve. the mystery?

b Major Sholto was an officer and a .... from a good British family.

c A .... is a small gun that you can shoot six times without stopping.

d The big house on the plan has several .... and a lot of rooms.

e There are four black .... on the plan.

f They saw the .... showing the way to the Lyceum and followed it.

g The street .... give a strange light in the fog.

h The small man .... the horses, and the cab starts moving.

i After some time they arrive outside the third house in an .... street.

j The front door of the house is opened by an Indian ....

GUESS WHAT

What happens in the next chapter? Tick the boxes.　　　　**Yes**　　**No**

a Miss Morstan meets an old family friend. ☐ ☐

b Miss Morstan learns that her father is dead. ☐ ☐

c Major Sholto's son explains why he has brought them to his house. ☐ ☐

d Sholto's son tries to kill Miss Morstan. ☐ ☐

e Miss Morstan learns how her father died. ☐ ☐

f Holmes says that Sholto is a murderer. ☐ ☐

Chapter three

Mr Thaddeus Sholto

We followed the Indian along a dark, dirty passage and came to a big wooden door. The servant opened it and we looked into a brightly lit room. A small, bald man stood in front of us in the strange, yellow light. He was a very ugly little man with bad teeth and thin lips. He looked about thirty years old.

'I am your servant, Miss Morstan,' he said again and again in his strange, high voice. 'Please come in. My house, I hope, is a special place among these poor streets of south London.'

It was true that we were all surprised by the room. While everything in the rest of the house looked old and broken, everything here was expensive and beautiful. The **curtains** were heavy and lovely to look at, and the carpet was thick under our feet. Everywhere there were valuable **paintings** and **vases**. A beautiful lamp burned in the middle of the room and gave out a sweet smell.

curtains people close these in front of windows at night, to stop people looking in

painting a picture, done with different colours and brushes

vase a container that people put flowers in

'My name is Thaddeus Sholto, Mr Thaddeus Sholto,' the man went on. He smiled as he spoke and he moved his hands, which were held closely together, all the time. 'You are Miss Morstan, of course, and these gentlemen?'

'This is Mr Sherlock Holmes,' replied Miss Morstan, 'and this is Dr Watson.'

'A doctor!' cried Sholto in excitement. 'Dr Watson, could you please listen to my heart? I really feel quite ill. I'm a little worried.'

I listened to his heart, but I could find no problem with it, although he was shaking with fear.

'You seem to be in good health,' I informed him. 'There's no reason to be worried.'

'Thank you, doctor,' he said. 'I've worried about my heart for a long time. I'm sorry that your father didn't take more care of *his* heart, Miss Morstan. With more care, perhaps he would still be alive and with us today.'

His careless words made me angry. Miss Morstan's face went very white, and she sat down.

'So he's dead,' she said. 'I knew it.'

'I can tell you everything,' Sholto went on, 'and I *will* tell you everything, although my brother Bartholomew won't be happy. I'm pleased that you've brought your friends with you because that means there are four of us against my brother. But it's very important that no one else knows about this.'

'Don't worry,' said Holmes, 'I won't tell anyone about this and I'm sure Dr Watson and Miss Morstan will say nothing.'

We said nothing but both **nodded** our heads to show that we agreed.

'Excellent!' he replied. 'Excellent! Would you like a glass of wine, Miss Morstan? No? I hope that it won't trouble you if I smoke. I feel a little **nervous**.'

He lit a cigarette and we sat down around him on the floor with our legs crossed.

nod to move your head up and down

nervous a little afraid

'When I decided to write to you,' he began, 'I didn't give this address because I feared that you might bring the police with you. That's why I asked my man to meet you at the Lyceum. I told him not to speak to you if he was worried. I don't like the police, you see. I find them very unpleasant. My life here is very quiet. As you can see, I have a strong interest in paintings and I love beautiful things.'

'Excuse me, Mr Sholto,' said Miss Morstan, 'but I am here because I think you can tell me about my father's death. It's late, so please tell me everything you know.'

'We must go to Norwood to see my brother, Bartholomew,' Sholto replied. 'He's very cross with me now. We argued last night because he's angry that I wrote to you, Miss Morstan. He's a dangerous man when he's angry, I can tell you.'

'Perhaps we should go to Norwood now,' I said, looking at my watch.

'We can't go now,' Sholto laughed loudly. 'I must tell you the story first. I'm sure you've realized my father was once Major John Sholto of the Indian army. Eleven years ago he retired and came to live at Norwood in a house called Pondicherry Lodge. He'd made a lot of money in India and had come back to England with a large number of Indian servants. He bought a big house and enjoyed a good life there. My brother, Bartholomew, and I were his only children.

'When Captain Morstan disappeared, we read the story in the newspaper. Because we knew that he'd been a friend of our father's, we talked about it with him. Together we wondered what had happened to the Captain. We never thought for a moment our father was the one person who knew. After Morstan's story was in the paper, Father was too frightened to go out alone and he always kept two **bodyguards** with him. We never understood why, but he became **terrified** of men with wooden legs. Some eight years ago he shot a black-haired man with a wooden leg who came to the house. The poor

bodyguard a man whose job is to protect someone

terrified very frightened

16

man was from the town nearby and was only trying to sell things that he'd made. Bartholomew and I had to pay him a lot of money to stop him going to the police. Now, at last, we understand why our father acted in this strange way, and I'll tell you the story:

Early in 1882 he received a letter from India, which made him very worried. When he opened it at the breakfast table, his face went quite white. We never found out what he had read in the letter, but as he held it in his hand that morning I could see it was short and that the writing was difficult to read. My father had been sick for many years, but now he became seriously ill. One day, at the end of April, his doctor told us that he was dying. But there was something that he wanted to tell us before he died.

My brother and I went into his bedroom. He was lying in bed and **breathing** heavily. He asked us to lock the door and come to him. Then, in a voice full of pain, he spoke.

breathe to make air move into and out of your body through your nose and mouth

17

'There's one thing I must tell you,' he said, 'I've acted very badly towards Morstan's daughter. I've kept all the **treasure** for myself and given none of it to the girl. Half of it should be hers, but I'm not a man that likes to give money away to anyone and I've enjoyed keeping all the treasure here at Pondicherry Lodge. When I'm dead, you must send Miss Morstan her half of the treasure, but not before.

'I'll tell you how her father died,' he went on. 'He'd had a weak heart for many years, although he never spoke about it. I was the only person who knew. When we were together in India, we'd **acquired** the treasure. I'd brought it back to England and when Morstan arrived, he came to see me to ask for his half. He walked here from the station. But we argued about how we should **divide** the treasure between us. Morstan became very angry, jumped out of his chair, and suddenly fell to the floor, his face quite grey. He cut his head badly on the treasure **chest** and I saw immediately that he was dead.

'I didn't know what to do. I wanted to call the police, but I feared they'd think I'd murdered him. Also, I didn't want anyone to find out about the treasure. As Morstan had told me no one knew that he'd come to see me, I decided no one should ever find out.

'My servant helped me to **bury** the body and a few days later I read in the newspapers that Captain Morstan had disappeared. You must understand that I didn't actually kill my friend, although it was wrong of me to hide his body and to keep all the treasure for myself. That's why you must now give Miss Morstan her half of the treasure. The treasure is hidden in –'

At that moment his face suddenly changed. His eyes became wild and he looked terrified. 'Don't let him in!' he cried. 'Please don't let him in!' Bartholomew and I turned to look at the bedroom window. There we saw

treasure
something expensive, for example gold, silver or valuable stones

acquire to get

divide to give parts of something to two or more people

chest a large box

bury to put a dead body under ground

a terrible hairy face with frightening red eyes, staring into the room from the darkness outside. We ran to the window but, when we got there, the man had disappeared. We returned to our father's bedside, but he was dead.

That night we searched the garden but we found only a single **footprint** in the mud under the window. We went to bed with heavy hearts that night. In the morning we found the window of my father's room open. Someone had searched his cupboards and boxes, and on his chest there was a piece of paper with the words 'The Sign of Four'. We never knew who had entered the house that night, and the words meant nothing to us.

The little man stopped to smoke some more and sat in silence for a few minutes. We were all thinking about the story that he had told us. Miss Morstan was, of course, very saddened by the news of her father's death. I offered her a glass of water, which she accepted.

Finally Thaddeus Sholto continued his story.

'For weeks and months my brother, Bartholomew, and I looked everywhere for the treasure, but without success. We weren't poor, but with the treasure we would be very rich. That's why I wanted to make sure that you would receive your half, Miss Morstan, as our father wished. Sadly, Bartholomew disagreed and we argued. I decided to leave Pondicherry Lodge and came to live here.

'Yesterday I heard that my brother had found the treasure, and that's why I wrote to you, Miss Morstan. Now we can drive to Norwood and ask Bartholomew for our part of the treasure. He knows that we're coming, but I must tell you that he isn't happy.'

'It's late,' said Holmes. 'And I think we should go to Norwood now. Our cab is still waiting outside. Thank you for your story, Mr Sholto. I'm sure this will be an interesting night.'

footprint a mark that your foot or shoe makes on the ground or floor

READING CHECK

1 Correct nine more mistakes in the chapter summary.

An Indian servant takes Holmes, Watson and Miss Morstan along a ~~bright~~ _dark_ passage to a room, where a short, handsome man is waiting for them. He looks about fifty years old. The man introduces himself as Major Sholto's father, Thaddeus Sholto. He explains that Captain Morstan died by accident after an argument with Major Sholto about some money which they had acquired in India. Sholto and his friend buried Captain Morstan's body and said nothing to the police. Sholto tells Thaddeus and his cousin Bartholomew about Captain Morstan's death and the American treasure. Thaddeus goes on to explain how he and his brother searched the house for a dark hairy man, but found only a finger-print. Now, after some time, Bartholomew has found the treasure. Miss Morstan says that they must go to Bartholomew's house to ask for their part of the treasure.

2 Put the sentences in order. Number them 1–7.

a ☐ Captain Morstan disappears.

b ☐ 1 Major Sholto retires and comes to live at Pondicherry Lodge.

c ☐ Sholto receives a letter from India.

d ☐ Sholto has a terrible surprise when a strange face appears at his bedroom window.

e ☐ Sholto dies.

f ☐ Sholto tells his sons to give some of the treasure to Miss Morstan.

g ☐ Sholto becomes ill.

WORD WORK

Find the words in the lamp to complete the sentences.

a Have you got a .....*vase*..... to put these flowers in? They'll die if they don't get some water soon.

b Don't be .... I'm not going to hurt you. I'm just going to look at that tooth.

c The .... in front of the windows were heavy and beautiful.

d They found some interesting paper in the old .... when they opened it.

e Major Sholto kept two .... with him to save him from danger.

f It isn't easy to .... this cake into five pieces, so I'll cut it into six and someone can have two pieces.

g The Mona Lisa – which is kept in the Louvre in Paris – is the most famous .... in the world.

h My sister was .... when she saw the new Frankenstein film.

i With his hand over her mouth and nose, she couldn't .... very easily.

j We .... to show that we agreed with his idea.

seva

renusov

stainruc

thesc

drugadobys

eviddi

inagpint

reftideri

hetrabe

doddne

GUESS WHAT

What happens in the next chapter? Tick three boxes.

a ☐ Holmes and Watson arrive at Pondicherry Lodge with Miss Morstan and Thaddeus Sholto.

b ☐ A man with a wooden leg opens the door at Pondicherry Lodge.

c ☐ Thaddeus Sholto kills his brother.

d ☐ Thaddeus Sholto finds his brother dead.

e ☐ Holmes and Watson discover a secret room under the roof.

f ☐ Holmes is attacked by a child.

Chapter four

Pondicherry Lodge

We all got into the cab, and the driver took us quickly to Norwood. As we travelled, Thaddeus Sholto spoke without stopping in his high voice.

'My brother, Bartholomew, is a clever man,' he began. 'He realized the treasure was somewhere indoors, so he **measured** all the rooms and passages. He discovered there must be a **space** somewhere at the top of the house. So he made a hole in the ceiling of our father's bedroom, and that's how he found the secret room under the roof where the treasure was hidden. He brought the chest down through the hole and opened it. He thinks it's worth at least **half a million** pounds.'

Neither Holmes nor I had **expected** the treasure to be worth so much, and I could see that Miss Morstan was also very surprised. This would make a great difference to her life. I wanted to be happy for her, but my heart felt very heavy. I managed to say that this was excellent news, but then I fell silent and I heard nothing more that Sholto said. Finally we arrived at Pondicherry Lodge. The driver got down and opened the door of the cab.

It was nearly eleven o'clock. We'd left the fog of the great **city** behind, and it was now a warm and pleasant night. A light wind blew from the west and heavy clouds moved slowly across the sky. Thaddeus Sholto took one of the lamps from the cab and we walked towards the house.

Pondicherry Lodge stood in a very large garden. There was a high wall around the house with broken glass on top. There was only one door in the wall and this was heavy and made of dark wood. Thaddeus Sholto knocked three times.

'Who's there?' asked a deep voice.

'Don't you recognize my knock?' replied Sholto.

We heard the sound of a key in the lock, and the door was

measure to find out how big something is

space an empty part of something

half a million 500, 000

expect to think that something will happen

city (*plural* **cities**) a big and important town

opened by a short, ugly man with small, grey eyes.

'Mr Thaddeus!' he said. 'But who are these people? Mr Bartholomew said nothing about other people.'

'I'm surprised,' said Sholto. 'I told my brother last night I'd bring some friends with me.'

'He told me nothing,' the man said, but he let us in.

He closed the door behind us and we followed a path through the garden, which had no flowers or trees in it, and walked towards Pondicherry Lodge. The house was **enormous**, but square and very ugly. It was dark and silent.

'That's strange,' said Sholto. 'There's no light in my brother's room although he knows about our visit.'

'But there's a light in that window by the door,' I said.

'That's Mrs Bernstone's room,' Sholto explained. 'She's the housekeeper. She'll be able to tell us where my brother is.'

At that moment we all heard the sound of a woman screaming. We looked at Sholto.

'That's her,' he said, 'Mrs Bernstone. Wait here.'

He ran to the door and knocked three times. It was opened by a tall old woman, who was clearly happy to see him.

'Mr Thaddeus,' she cried. 'I'm so pleased you're here.'

The door closed behind the housekeeper and Thaddeus Sholto. We still had the lamp with us, and Holmes used it to look more closely at the garden.

'What are those?' said Miss Morstan, looking at the holes in the grass.

'Mr Bartholomew Sholto has been digging here for the last six years,' said Holmes. 'But when he finally found the treasure, it was in the house, not the garden!'

Just then, the door opened and Thaddeus Sholto ran out. He looked very frightened.

'Come in!' he cried in his high voice. 'There's something wrong with Bartholomew.'

We followed him into the housekeeper's room.

enormous very big

'Mr Bartholomew has locked the door to his room,' the old woman explained, 'and he refuses to let me in. I've waited all day because he often likes to be alone, but an hour ago I began to fear something bad had happened. I looked through the keyhole into his room and I saw him. The look on his face was terrible! I can't go back upstairs, Mr Thaddeus!'

Holmes, with the lamp in his hand, went upstairs, and I and Thaddeus Sholto, who was shaking with fear, followed him. The detective stopped several times to look carefully at the stairs. He moved slowly and we waited patiently behind him. At the top of the stairs we found ourselves in a long passage. There was an enormous Indian painting on one wall, and on the other side of the passage there were three doors.

The third door was Bartholomew's room. Holmes knocked loudly on it, but there was no answer. Holmes then tried to open the door, but it was locked. He **crouched down** and looked through the keyhole. Immediately he stood up again. It was clear that he was very worried.

'This is serious, Watson,' he said. 'See for yourself.'

I crouched down to look through the hole and saw something terrible beyond it. Light from the moon entered the room

crouch down to bend your knees so that your body is close to the ground

through the window and in that light I could see an unmoving face – the face of Thaddeus Sholto – with the strangest most frightening smile fixed on it! I turned to make sure that Thaddeus Sholto was still with us, and then I realized – Bartholomew was Thaddeus's **twin** brother.

'What can we do, Holmes?' I asked.

'We must enter the room,' my friend answered, then threw himself against the door. But the lock was a strong one, and the door refused to open. So Holmes and I threw ourselves against it together and this time it opened. We found ourselves in Bartholomew Sholto's room. It was a small **laboratory**, full of different things in bottles on the table and on the floor around the edges of the room. One of the bottles on the floor was broken, and some smelly black **tar** was coming out of it.

In one corner of the room there was a **ladder**, and at the top of it there was a hole in the ceiling. At the bottom there was a **rope**. At the table on a wooden chair sat Bartholomew Sholto. We saw at once that he had been dead for some hours.

His hand lay on the table next to a sheet of paper. On the paper we read the words, 'The Sign of Four'.

'What can it mean?' I asked.

twin one of a pair of brothers or sisters who are born on the same day

laboratory a room where someone puts things together and examines what happens to them

tar this is soft, black and smelly; we put it on roads and there is some in cigarettes too

ladder you use this for climbing up or down tall buildings or other things

rope a very thick, strong string

'It means murder,' Holmes replied. 'Look at this.'

He showed me a long, dark **thorn** in the dead man's skin, just above the ear.

'It's a **poisoned** thorn, Watson,' he went on. 'You can take it out, but be very careful.'

I took the thorn between my finger and my thumb. There was a very small drop of blood on Bartholomew's face, where it had entered the skin.

Suddenly I remembered Thaddeus Sholto, who was still standing behind us. He looked terrified.

'Are you all right?' I asked.

'The treasure has gone!' he cried. 'Someone has stolen it! I helped my brother bring it down last night. I was the last person to see him. I left him here and I heard him lock the door as I went downstairs.'

'What time was that?' asked Holmes, suddenly interested.

'Ten o'clock,' replied Sholto. 'And now he's dead! The police will think I killed my brother. I'm sure they will! Mr Holmes, you don't think that I'm a murderer, do you?'

'I'm sure you didn't kill your brother,' said the detective, 'and I **suggest** that you go to the police station immediately and tell them what happened. Watson and I will wait here.'

At Holmes's words, Sholto became a little calmer.

'Thank you, Mr Holmes, I'll go now,' he said, and with that he went down the stairs and left the house.

Holmes turned to me.

'Watson,' he said, 'we have perhaps half an hour. Sit down. I have work to do. First, I'd like to know how the murderer entered and left the room. No one has opened the door since last night. But what about the window?'

Holmes crossed the room and looked carefully at the window.

'Yes!' he said. 'Someone has entered the room here. It rained a little last night and look, Watson, here's a footprint and a round, muddy **mark**. And here's another. Very interesting.'

thorn something small and sharp that grows on a plant and can hurt you

poisoned with something on it that can kill you if it gets into your body

suggest to say that something is a good idea

mark something dirty of a different colour that you see on something

'That isn't a footprint, Holmes,' I said.

'No,' he agreed, 'It's the mark of a wooden leg.'

'The man with the wooden leg!' I cried. 'Do you remember? Thaddeus Sholto told us that his father was terrified of men with wooden legs.'

'Of course,' my friend replied, 'but this man with a wooden leg didn't work alone. Could you climb this wall?'

I looked out of the open window. The moon shone on the side of the house.

'Impossible,' I said.

'Impossible without help,' answered Holmes, 'but with a friend at the window and a rope you could do it. A man with a wooden leg could do it.'

'Perhaps,' I agreed, 'but how then did this friend enter the room? The door was locked.'

'Think, Watson,' said Holmes. 'He didn't come through the door and he didn't come through the window.'

I looked around the room and then cried, 'He came down the ladder from the room under the roof!'

'Of course,' Holmes agreed. 'it's the only possible way that's left. Let's now **examine** the secret room, Watson.'

I followed my friend up the ladder and into the room under the roof. Holmes held up the lamp, and we looked around us. We were in a small, empty room. The roof was high enough for us to stand, but it was a **tiny** space.

'See here, Watson,' said Holmes, 'there's a door, which opens onto the roof. This is how our man came into the house!'

He put down the lamp and once again I saw a look of surprise on his face. I soon understood why. On the floor were some little footprints.

'Holmes!' I cried. 'Is it possible that our murderer is a child?'

'No,' he replied, 'not a child.'

'Then how do you explain those tiny footprints?' I asked.

'Everything will become clear, Watson. Let's go down.'

examine to look carefully at something

tiny very small

READING CHECK

Tick the correct answers.

a What happens in the cab on the way to Norwood?
  1 ☐ Miss Morstan talks about her father.
  2 ☑ Thaddeus Sholto speaks about the treasure.
  3 ☐ Holmes and Watson discuss their work.

b Why does Thaddeus Sholto run out of Pondicherry Lodge?
  1 ☐ Because he can't find the housekeeper.
  2 ☐ Because there's something wrong with Bartholomew Sholto.
  3 ☐ Because someone attacks him.

c What does Holmes see through the keyhole of Bartholomew Sholto's room?
  1 ☐ The housekeeper's body.
  2 ☐ Bartholomew Sholto's body.
  3 ☐ Bartholomew Sholto's face with a strange smile.

d What do Holmes and Watson find out in Bartholomew Sholto's room?
  1 ☐ That Bartholomew Sholto has been murdered.
  2 ☐ That Bartholomew Sholto has hidden the treasure.
  3 ☐ That Thaddeus Sholto is a murderer.

e Who came into the room through the window?
  1 ☐ Thaddeus Sholto.
  2 ☐ A man with a wooden leg.
  3 ☐ Someone with tiny feet.

f How did this person's friend enter the room?
  1 ☐ Through the door.
  2 ☐ Through the window.
  3 ☐ Through the roof.

WORD WORK

1 These words don't match the pictures. Correct them.

a ~~measure~~
  thorn
b ladder
c city
d twins
e laboratory
f thorn

2 Find words in the rope to complete the sentences.

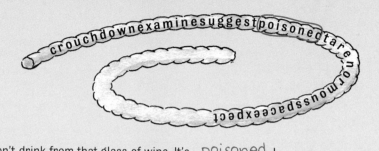

a Don't drink from that glass of wine. It's ..poisoned !

b The new black .... on the road shone under the light of the sun.

c Your cat isn't just big, it's really ....!

d The door's very low. You must .... when you go through.

e Where can we put the milk? There isn't any ...., in the fridge.

f Doctor, can you .... my eye. I think that there's something wrong with it.

g Can I .... that we open the window? It's very hot in here.

h Fred's late back from lunch again, but I .... him to be here soon.

GUESS WHAT

What happens in the next chapter? Tick the boxes.

a Thaddeus Sholto returns to Pondicherry Lodge with …

 1 ☐ Inspector Lestrade

 2 ☐ Miss Morstan

 3 ☐ Dr Watson

b The police arrest…

 1 ☐ Mrs Bernstone

 2 ☐ Miss Morstan

 3 ☐ Thaddeus Sholto

c Holmes sends Watson to find …

 1 ☐ a policeman

 2 ☐ a dog

 3 ☐ the treasure

Chapter five

An Early Arrest

We climbed back down into Bartholomew Sholto's room, where Holmes began to search the floor.

'At last we have some good luck,' he said, standing up. 'Look, Watson, at these footprints. Our little visitor has **trodden** in this tar here. Can you smell it?'

I agreed that there was a strong smell.

'Then we have him!' cried Holmes. 'I know a dog that will be able to follow this smell and take us to him.'

At that moment the police arrived, with Thaddeus Sholto.

'Inspector Lestrade,' said Holmes. 'Good evening.'

Inspector Lestrade of Scotland Yard gave us a long look while Thaddeus Sholto looked very uncomfortable.

'Good evening, Mr Holmes, Dr Watson,' said Lestrade at last. 'Perhaps you can tell me what's happened here?'

'Well,' Holmes began, but the Inspector stopped him.

'Or can I tell *you* what's happened this time, Mr Holmes,' he went on. 'We have a dead body in a locked room. Some valuable treasure, I understand, has disappeared. Mr Thaddeus Sholto was with his brother last night and is now very excited.'

He turned to Sholto.

'Did you kill your brother?'

Thaddeus Sholto's face went white. He opened his mouth, but no words, came out.

'Inspector Lestrade,' said Holmes, 'you should know that we found this poisoned thorn in the dead man's skin and this strange paper with the words, 'The Sign of Four'.'

'That changes nothing!' Lestrade replied. 'Do you have anything to say, Mr Sholto?'

The poor man tried to speak, but again no words came.

'Thaddeus Sholto, I am arresting you for the murder of your brother, Bartholomew Sholto. Sergeant Judd, take him away.'

tread (*past* **trod**, **trodden**) to walk or step in something

Judd took
Sholto by the arm
and they left the room.

'I think we have our killer,
Mr Holmes,' Lestrade went on.

'You're wrong, Inspector,' Holmes replied, 'but I can give you the name of one of the two men who were in this room last night. It's Jonathan Small. He isn't a very clever man. Although he's tall and has a wooden leg, he moves quickly. He's about fifty years old, an Englishman, but with skin burnt dark by the sun. He's spent time in prison.'

'And the other man?' asked Lestrade, who was clearly surprised by all the information that my friend had given him.

'He's a very strange person,' said Holmes. 'I hope to **introduce** you to them both very soon, Inspector. Good night.'

I followed Holmes from the room. At the bottom of the stairs he turned to me.

'Watson, you must take Miss Morstan home. It's very late.'

'Of course,' I agreed. 'And then?'

Holmes took a piece of paper from his pocket and wrote an address on it.

'And then go to this house and ask for the dog Toby. Bring him here to me as quickly as possible. While you're away I'll talk to Mrs Bernstone and the Indian servant. They may have useful information for us.'

introduce to bring people together for the first time by saying their names and something about them

candle it burns
and gives light; in
the past people
used them to see
at night

attack to start
biting or hitting
someone

Although my friend's plan was not clear to me at that time, I did not ask him to explain. I left him in the passage and went to find Miss Morstan.

We travelled by cab to Camberwell in south London, where we said goodnight. I felt very sad. There was so much that I wanted to say to her, but I knew that I mustn't. She might soon be a rich woman, and I didn't want her to think that my interest was in her money.

On the journey from Camberwell I thought about everything that had happened. The mystery of Pondicherry Lodge and its treasure seemed a very dark one.

The address Holmes had given me was in a row of dirty houses in the poorest part of Lambeth, just south of the River Thames. I asked the driver to stop, and got out of the cab. I had to knock several times before the door opened. Suddenly I saw an angry face, which was lit by a **candle**, looking out.

'Go away!' said the man. 'It's the middle of the night. If you don't go away, my dogs will **attack** you.'

'But I want one of your dogs,' I tried to explain. 'Mr Sherlock Holmes has sent me.'

Immediately the man's face changed.

'Oh. Any friend of Mr Sherlock's is welcome. Come in!'

I found myself in a tiny room with lots of dogs of all kinds. The man lit a lamp and introduced himself.

'Benedict Sherman,' he said, and held out his hand.

'John Watson,' I replied, shaking it. 'I've come for Toby.'

I could see now that the room contained not only dogs but chickens. Five or six birds were sitting on the table.

Sherman introduced me to Toby, a large, ugly animal, and I took the dog out to my cab. I thanked Mr Sherman and waved goodbye to him as we drove away.

It was three o'clock in the morning when I returned to Pondicherry Lodge. I found Holmes at the front door.

'Good morning, Watson,' he said. 'I see you've found Toby. Lestrade has gone. He arrested not only Mr Thaddeus Sholto but also all the servants in the house. We're alone here, Watson, except for **Sergeant** Judd, who's upstairs. Come in.'

We left the dog in the garden and climbed the stairs to Bartholomew Sholto's room. Judd was asleep in an armchair.

'We mustn't wake the sergeant up, Watson,' said Holmes with a smile. 'Follow me.'

We climbed the ladder to the space in the roof, where my friend held his lamp above some footprints on the floor.

'What do you notice?' he asked.

'The footprints are very small,' I answered. 'They were probably made by a child or a small woman. But there's a big space between each toe.'

'Very good,' said Holmes. 'Now come to the window. Can you see the tar here? This is where he put his foot. The tar has a strong smell and I'm sure Toby will be able to follow him. I myself climbed out of this window and down the **drainpipe** while you were away, Watson, and on the ground I found this little bag. It contains thorns like the poisoned thorn we found in Bartholomew Sholto's skin. I'm sure our murderer dropped this when he left.'

'Deadly!' I said, looking carefully at the thorns.

sergeant
an important policeman

drainpipe
something long and round that carries water away from the roof of a building

33

'But not to us, Watson,' my friend replied. 'Now let's go down and find Toby. His work begins now.'

The dog was waiting impatiently for us. Soon we were running behind him through the dark streets of Norwood.

'We're lucky it hasn't rained much,' said Holmes. 'Rain makes Toby's work very difficult.'

I was surprised the dog knew where he was going, but I could see Holmes had worked with Toby many times before.

'Tell me, Holmes,' I said as we ran, 'how were you able to describe the man with the wooden leg to Lestrade?'

'Elementary, Watson,' my friend replied. 'Two army officers who are working at a prison in the Andaman Islands discover an important secret about buried treasure. An Englishman called Jonathan Small draws a map for them. We saw his name on the map that Miss Morstan showed us. He'd signed the paper for himself and for his **associates**: 'The Sign of Four'. With this map, one of the officers finds the treasure and brings it to England. Why didn't Small get the treasure himself? Because he and his associates were all in prison.'

'Are you sure about this, Holmes?' I asked him.

'It's the only explanation,' he replied. 'Major Sholto lives happily with his treasure in Norwood. Then one day a letter arrives from India, and frightens him. Why?'

'Because the letter told him that Small and his associates were now free men,' I suggested.

'Good, Watson. Yes, they'd probably escaped. He's now terrified of a man with a wooden leg. We know this because Thaddeus Sholto told us that he once shot a man like that from the nearby town who came to the house. He clearly thought that the man was Jonathan Small. Only one of the names on the map is the name of a white man, so I think we can be sure that Jonathan Small and the man with the wooden leg are the same person.'

I agreed that this seemed probable.

associate
someone that you often spend time with or are in business with

34

'Well, now let's think about Jonathan Small,' my friend went on. 'He comes to England for two reasons: he wants the treasure, but he also wants to **punish** Sholto for stealing it. He finds out where the Major lives, but he can't find the treasure. Suddenly he hears that Sholto is on his deathbed.'

'And only Sholto knows where the treasure is!'

'Very good, Watson,' Holmes replied. 'Small arrives at the window of the Major's room, but sees his two sons, Bartholomew and Thaddeus, by the dying man's bed. So he doesn't enter the room then, but comes back during the night after Sholto has died and searches his papers. He finds nothing, but leaves a card with the words, 'The Sign of Four'.'

'But why, Holmes?' I asked.

'To frighten the Major's sons, perhaps,' Holmes suggested, and then continued.

'After that I think Small watches Bartholomew Sholto searching the garden for the treasure. When Bartholomew discovers the room under the roof, Small has a problem. With his wooden leg he can't climb up to the room, so he brings with him a strange associate. But the associate puts his foot in the tar and that's why you and I are now moving so quickly through the streets of Norwood with Toby.'

'So Small himself didn't kill Bartholomew Sholto,' I said.

'That's right,' Holmes agreed. 'His associate is clearly a dangerous man. My revolver is ready, Watson.'

punish to hurt someone because they have done something wrong

READING CHECK

1 Put these sentences in the correct order. Number them 1–6.

a ☐ Holmes and Watson follow Toby through the streets of Norwood.

b ☐ Inspector Lestrade arrives with Thaddeus Sholto.

c ☐ Watson goes to Lambeth to find the dog Toby.

d ☐ Inspector Lestrade arrests Thaddeus Sholto.

e ☐ 1 Holmes and Watson search Bartholomew Sholto's room.

f ☐ Watson takes Miss Morstan home to Camberwell.

2 Are these sentences true or false? Tick the boxes.

		True	False
a	Holmes finds black footprints in the room.	☑	☐
b	Lestrade thinks that Thaddeus Sholto killed his brother.	☐	☐
c	Jonathan Small has a wooden leg.	☐	☐
d	Watson and Miss Morstan take the train to Camberwell.	☐	☐
e	Watson is interested in Miss Morstan because he thinks she will be rich.	☐	☐
f	Watson finds the dog Toby in a poor part of Lambeth.	☐	☐
g	Watson climbs down a drainpipe at Pondicherry Lodge.	☐	☐
h	Holmes thinks that Jonathan Small's associate killed Bartholomew Sholto.	☐	☐

WORD WORK

1 Find seven more words from Chapter 5 in the word square.

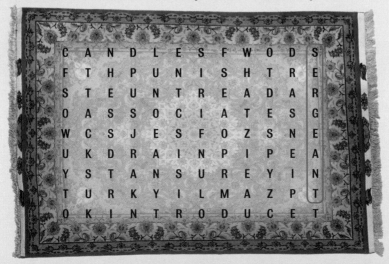

```
C A N D L E S F W O D S
F T H P U N I S H T R E
S T E U N T R E A D A R
O A S S O C I A T E S G
W C S J E S F O Z S N E
U K D R A I N P I P E A
Y S T A N S U R E Y I N
T U R K Y I L M A Z P T
O K I N T R O D U C E T
```

2 Use the words from Activity 1 to complete these sentences.

a My uncle was a police ...*sergeant*. for many years.

b The thief climbed up the .... and through the bedroom window.

c I'm going to .... you, you bad boy. You won't watch any TV tonight.

d There are fifty .... on my birthday cake because I'm fifty this year.

e Our dog often .... the postman when he brings letters to our front door.

f We believe that the criminal worked alone, without any ....

g Did you .... in some paint? Your shoes are all blue!

h Uncle John, can I .... you to my friend, Jane.

GUESS WHAT

What happens in the next chapter? Make four sentences with these phrases to find out.

a	e	i
Holmes and Watson follow	street boys	to find the missing boat.
b	**f**	**j**
A woman's	about Thaddeus's arrest	to the River Thames.
c	**g**	**k**
Holmes asks some	husband has disappeared	by Inspector Lestrade.
d	**h**	**l**
Watson reads	Toby	with his boat.

Chapter six

The Aurora

suburbs the outer parts of a town, where people live

mile 1.61 kilometres

for hire can be borrowed after you pay something for it

steam launch a fast boat that is powered by steam from burning coal

We followed Toby through the **suburbs** for several **miles** and the sun was coming up when the dog finally stopped beside the River Thames. Here he stood, looking at the water as it moved quickly towards the sea.

'What luck,' said Holmes. 'They've taken a boat.'

'Perhaps they used one of these,' I suggested, pointing at the six or seven boats that we could see on the river.

'Perhaps,' Holmes replied, 'Let's see what Toby thinks.'

We took the dog to each of the boats one after the other, but he showed no interest in any of them.

There was a small house beside the river and outside it there was a sign with these words on it:

MORDECAI SMITH
BOATS
FOR
HIRE
STEAM LAUNCH

My friend looked worried when he saw this.

'They're cleverer than I thought, Watson,' he said.

Just then the door of the house opened. A young boy ran out. His mother, a large woman with a red face, followed him.

'Come back!' she cried. 'I'll wash your face this morning if it's the last thing that I do!'

'Hello,' said Holmes to the boy. 'You're a fine young man. Is there anything you'd like?'

The child looked up at my friend in surprise.

'I'd like a shilling,' he said, 'please.'

'Of course,' Holmes agreed, taking a shilling from his pocket. 'You have a good boy here, Mrs Smith.'

The woman stopped to look at my friend as he spoke.

'He *is* a good boy,' she replied, 'usually. But he can be very difficult when my husband's away.'

'Is Mr Smith away at the moment?' asked Holmes. 'I was hoping to speak to him.'

'He went away yesterday morning,' she replied, 'and I'm quite worried about him, sir. He took the steam launch and he only had enough **coal** to travel a very short way. But he's been away for more than twenty-four hours now.'

'Could he buy more coal along the river?' Holmes suggested.

'I don't think so,' said Mrs Smith. 'And I don't like the man who went with him. He's been here before. He's got a wooden leg. This time he came in the middle of the night and I haven't seen my husband since then.'

'Are you sure it was the man with the wooden leg?' asked Holmes. 'You didn't see him, I suppose.'

'No, I didn't. But I know it was him,' the woman replied. 'I heard his wooden leg on the street when he walked away with my husband and my older boy, Jim.'

coal it is hard and black, and burns very well; people use it to make the fire that moves old ships and trains

'Well,' said Holmes 'I'm sorry to hear that, Mrs Smith. I very much wanted to hire your steam launch. So many people have told me that she's a good boat.'

'Yes,' Mrs Smith agreed. 'The *Aurora*'s a fine launch.'

'The *Aurora*,' said Holmes. 'Green, isn't she? And quite wide?'

'Oh no, sir,' the woman replied. 'The *Aurora* isn't wide, and she's black, not green.'

'Of course,' Holmes agreed. 'Black, not green. We must go, Mrs Smith. I hope that you'll have news of your husband soon. If I see him along the river, I'll tell him that you're worried. Goodbye.'

My friend and I then found a man with a boat, who took us across the river. When we reached the other side, Holmes turned to me.

'Well, Watson,' he asked. 'What should we do now?'

'I think we should hire another launch and go after the *Aurora*,' I suggested.

Holmes shook his head.

'There are too many places along the river for the *Aurora* to hide,' he said. 'We might spend days looking for her.'

'Then perhaps we should ask Inspector Lestrade for some help from Scotland Yard,' I replied.

'Not yet, Watson,' said my friend. 'I'd like to find Mr Jonathan Small for myself, if I can. No, let's take this cab here back to Baker Street and have some breakfast. We should also sleep for an hour or two.'

We got into the cab and were soon travelling north to Baker Street with the dog, Toby. On the way, Holmes asked the driver to stop at a post office. There he got down from the cab and, when he came back, he told me that he had sent a telegram.

'Do you remember the group of street boys who helped us once before, Watson?' he asked. 'I've sent a telegram to their **leader**. I'm sure he and the boys will be with us before we've finished breakfast.'

leader the most important one in a group

It was after eight o'clock when we arrived at 221B Baker Street. I was **exhausted** and went to have a bath. After this, and an excellent breakfast of coffee, toast and eggs, I felt better. Holmes drank only a cup of coffee and smoked a cigarette before showing me the morning newspaper.

'Look at this, Watson,' he smiled. 'Inspector Lestrade has been speaking to the reporters, I think.'

I took the newspaper from my friend and read the story.

STRANGE BUSINESS in Norwood

At about midnight last night Mr Bartholomew Sholto of Pondicherry Lodge, Norwood, was found dead in his room. The police think that he was murdered. We understand that some valuable treasure was stolen from the house. Mr Sholto's father, an army officer, had brought the treasure back from India.

Mr Sholto's body was found by Mr Sherlock Holmes, the detective, and his associate, Dr John Watson. They had come to Pondicherry Lodge with the dead man's brother, Mr Thaddeus Sholto.

By chance, Inspector Lestrade of Scotland Yard was at the police station in Norwood and he immediately went to the house. The Inspector quickly realized that someone had **committed** a serious crime and arrested Mr Thaddeus Sholto and three servants from the house. He saw that the murderer had entered the dead man's room from a secret space under the roof and not by the door or window, and understood that the murderer must be someone who knew Pondicherry Lodge very well. This newspaper feels that the people of London should again be grateful to Inspector Lestrade for his excellent work in arresting criminals so quickly.

I put down the newspaper.

'But this is stupid, Holmes!' I said.

'Of course,' my friend agreed, 'but it makes me smile.'

Just then we heard lots of high voices at our door.

exhausted very tired

commit to do a crime

READING CHECK

Choose the right words to finish these sentences.

a Holmes and Watson follow Toby for several . . .

   1 ☐ days.

   2 ☐ hours.

   3 ☑ miles.

b Mordecai Smith has . . .

   1 ☐ boats for sale.

   2 ☐ boats for hire.

   3 ☐ only one boat.

c Mrs Smith explains that her husband took . . .

   1 ☐ the steam launch.

   2 ☐ the car.

   3 ☐ a cab.

d Mordecai Smith left . . .

   1 ☐ alone.

   2 ☐ with a man with a wooden leg.

   3 ☐ with a young woman.

e Holmes and Watson travel back to Baker Street . . .

   1 ☐ by cab with Mrs Smith.

   2 ☐ by cab with Toby the dog.

   3 ☐ by train with Mordecai Smith.

f Holmes stops at a post office . . .

   1 ☐ to send a telegram.

   2 ☐ to post a letter.

   3 ☐ to buy some stamps.

g At 221B Baker Street Watson . . .

   1 ☐ sits down to read the newspaper.

   2 ☐ goes to bed.

   3 ☐ has a bath and then has breakfast.

WORD WORK

Find words in the boats to complete the sentences.

a Holmes and Watson follow the dog
through the ..*suburbs*..

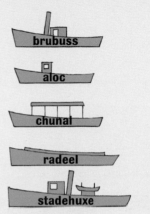

brubuss

b Can you bring in some more
c................. to put on the fire?

aloc

c Mordecai Smith has a steam
l................. for hire.

chunal

d Mustafa Kemal Ataturk was the
l................. of Turkey for many years.

radeel

e Watson is e................. when he gets
back to Baker Street.

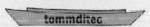

stadehuxe

f Lestrade thinks Thaddeus Sholto has
c................. a serious crime.

tommditec

GUESS WHAT

What happens in the next chapter? Match the people with the sentences.

Sherlock   Dr Watson   Mrs Hudson   Wiggins   Mordecai Smith
Holmes

a .... arrives at Baker Street with ten or more other boys.

b .... asks the Baker Street boys to find the *Aurora*.

c .... is not found.

d .... takes Toby back to his owner.

e .... is worried about Sherlock Holmes.

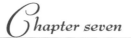

Chapter seven

The Baker Street Boys

'Who's making that terrible noise?' I asked in surprise.

Holmes put out his cigarette.

'The Baker Street boys, if I'm not wrong,' he answered calmly.

Mrs Hudson came in with a cross look on her face.

'The Baker Street boys for you, Mr Holmes,' she said.

Ten boys, most in dirty clothes and all without shoes, came into the room. They stood in a line, and looked at my friend and myself. Their leader, who was taller and older than the others, stepped forward.

'I got your message, sir,' he said to Holmes, 'and we came as quickly as we could.'

'Thank you, Wiggins,' Holmes replied. 'Now listen carefully, all of you. I want you to find a black steam launch called the *Aurora*. Her owner is Mr Mordecai Smith. She's somewhere on the river, but we have no idea where. One boy needs to wait by Smith's house at Millbank because the launch may come back. The rest of you should search both banks of the river and tell me as soon as you have news. Is that clear?'

'Yes, sir,' said Wiggins.

'I'll pay the same as before,' said Holmes, 'with a pound more for the boy who finds the boat. Here's your money for today.'

He gave each boy a coin, and they ran down the stairs at once and disappeared into Baker Street.

'If the launch is on the river, they'll find her,' said Holmes, standing up and lighting another cigarette. 'Those boys can go everywhere, see everything, listen to everyone. I'm sure one of them will find the *Aurora* today. So we must wait, Watson, because without Mr Mordecai Smith or his launch there's nothing we can do.'

'Are you going to bed, Holmes?' I asked.

My friend shook his head.

'I'm not tired, Watson. Work never makes me tired, but I always become exhausted when I have nothing to do. I'm going to smoke another cigarette or two and think about all this. Let's not forget that we're looking for a man with a wooden leg and his very strange associate. It really shouldn't be too difficult to find them.'

'Who *is* this associate, Holmes?' I wondered.

'There's no great mystery there,' Holmes replied. 'I don't know the man's name, of course, but I know a lot about him. He has very small feet and no spaces between his toes. He doesn't wear shoes and he climbs very well. He kills with poisoned thorns. The **natives** of the Andaman Islands are the smallest people in the world, and I understand they are also

native a person that was born and lives in a place

very ugly, with large heads and tiny hands and feet. They often kill strangers who come to their islands, and they're **cannibals**, too.'

'Friendly people, then!' I said.

'As I said, Watson, Jonathan Small's associate is a very dangerous person.'

Suddenly my friend looked worried.

'But you look exhausted, Watson. Why don't you sleep?'

'I *am* tired,' I agreed. 'Perhaps I will rest for a while.'

As I fell asleep in my chair, Sherlock Holmes was standing at the window looking down into Baker Street, playing his **violin**. I dreamed, of course, of Miss Mary Morstan.

I slept until the afternoon, and woke up like a new man. Holmes was sitting at the table, reading a book.

'You slept very deeply, Watson,' he said. 'I feared that our conversation would wake you up.'

'Has Wiggins come back, then?' I asked. 'I heard nothing.'

'He's just left,' Holmes replied, 'but he had no news for us. His boys have found nothing. I must say that I'm surprised and **disappointed**. Time is short.'

'Can I do anything?' I offered. 'I'm quite ready for another adventure after my sleep.'

'No, we can do nothing,' said Holmes. 'We can only wait. If we go out, Wiggins may return to find nobody here and there must be no unnecessary **delay**. You can do what you wish, Watson, but I must stay here.'

'Then I'll go to Camberwell,' I replied. 'Miss Morstan asked me to give her any news of our adventures, and although there's nothing we can do at the moment, I can tell her about Small and his associate, and about the *Aurora*.'

'Don't stay too long, Watson,' said my friend. 'We may have work to do later. Oh, and can you take Toby back on your way to Camberwell? His work for us is finished.'

I took the dog to the strange house where I had found him

cannibal a person who eats people

violin a musical instrument, made of wood with strings across it

disappointed unhappy because you don't get what you want

delay a time when you have to wait for something to happen

and paid his owner. Then I went on to Camberwell. Miss Morstan was quite tired after her adventures the night before, but she was very interested in my story.

'If we find the treasure,' I said, 'you'll be very rich, Mary.'

I was pleased to see she didn't seem **thrilled** by the idea.

'I'm thinking more about Mr Thaddeus,' she replied. 'He's a good man. We must do everything that we can to help him.'

Her words only made me love her more. I stayed in Camberwell talking for several hours and it was dark when I returned to Baker Street. My friend's book was on the table with his cigarette box, but Holmes himself had gone.

'Has Mr Holmes gone out?' I asked Mrs Hudson.

'No, sir. He's gone to his bedroom.'

Suddenly she spoke very quietly.

'I'm worried about him, sir. After you left, he walked and walked around this room for hours. Then I heard him **muttering** to himself in a strange way. Every time someone knocked on the front door he came to the top of the stairs and called down to me, "What's that, Mrs Hudson?" And now he's gone up to his room, but I can still hear him up there walking around. I hope that he isn't sick, sir.'

'I don't think that you need to worry too much, Mrs Hudson,' I replied. 'I've seen this before. He's thinking, that's all.'

'I hope that you're right, sir,' she said.

thrilled very excited

mutter to talk unclearly in a low, quiet voice

READING CHECK

Correct the mistakes in these sentences.

a Mrs Hudson introduces the Baker Street boys with a ~~happy~~ *cross* look on her face.

b The boys are dressed in clean clothes.

c Holmes explains that the *Aurora* is a green boat.

d Holmes tells the boys to search the streets.

e Jonathan Small's associate kills people with poisoned drinks.

f People from the Andaman Islands are very tall.

g Holmes falls asleep in his chair.

h Watson decides to visit Miss Morstan in Norwood.

i Miss Morstan is worried about Mordecai Smith.

j Watson talks to himself in a strange way.

LXXIV. — Iles Andaman. La rue des Bazars a Port Blair.

Grav. et imp. par Gillot.

WORD WORK

Correct the words in these sentences. They all come from Chapter 7.

a Holmes likes music and can play the **violent**. violin

b I was **disappeared** when I got five pounds for my birthday, not fifty. ....

c Nobody ever found his body. Perhaps **candidates** ate it. ....

d She felt really **grilled** when she won a holiday in Egypt. ....

e **Natures** of the Andaman Islands are ugly, says Holmes. ....

f There are **relays** to all trains today because of the bad weather. ....

g Mrs Hudson hears Holmes **guttering** to himself. ....

GUESS WHAT

What happens in the next chapter? Match the two parts of the sentences.

a Holmes spends the night

b Watson takes a cab to Camberwell

c Inspector Lestrade realizes that

d An old sailor brings Watson news of

e Holmes, Watson and Lestrade board

1 to report the latest news to Miss Morstan.

2 Mordecai Smith and the *Aurora*.

3 a police launch at Westminster.

4 walking around his bedroom.

5 Thaddeus did not murder his brother.

Chapter eight

The Old Sailor

During the long night that followed I heard my friend walking around his bedroom, and at breakfast the next morning I could see that he had not slept at all.

'Are you all right, Holmes?' I asked. 'I heard you moving around your room in the night.'

'I didn't sleep,' my friend replied. 'I spent the night thinking about our problem. I know the men, I know the launch, everything, but I can get no news. The Baker Street boys have searched both sides of the river, but they've found nothing. And Mrs Smith has no news of her husband. It's a real mystery.'

'Is it possible that the launch is no longer in the centre of London but has travelled up the river?' I wondered.

'I had the same idea,' said Holmes. 'Some of the boys are now searching both banks of the river as far up as Richmond. If they find anything, Wiggins will come and tell us.'

But the day passed and we did not see Wiggins. Holmes and I read the newspapers, which contained more stories about the death in Norwood. They all reported that Thaddeus Sholto was the probable murderer of his brother, Bartholomew, and described Inspector Lestrade as a great detective.

In the evening I took a cab to Camberwell to give the latest news to Miss Morstan. When I returned to Baker Street my friend was strangely silent. He answered my questions with single words and smoked cigarette after cigarette.

I woke early to find him by my bed, dressed as a sailor.

'I'm going down the river, Watson,' he said. 'I've been thinking about this all night, and it's the only thing to do.'

'I'll come with you,' I offered immediately.

'No,' he replied. 'You must stay here. We may have news from young Wiggins during the day. Please open any messages or telegrams that arrive and decide what to do if news comes.

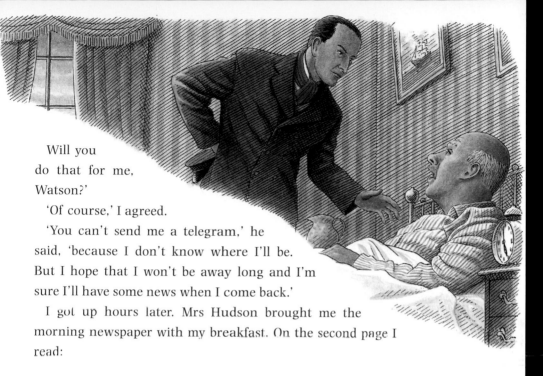

   Will you
do that for me,
Watson?'

   'Of course,' I agreed.

   'You can't send me a telegram,' he
said, 'because I don't know where I'll be.
But I hope that I won't be away long and I'm
sure I'll have some news when I come back.'

   I got up hours later. Mrs Hudson brought me the
morning newspaper with my breakfast. On the second page I
read:

Strange Death in Norwood

The mystery around the death of Mr Bartholomew Sholto in Norwood, south London, has become deeper. It is now clear that Mr Sholto was not murdered by his brother, Thaddeus, who is now a free man. Inspector Lestrade of Scotland Yard has told this newspaper that he hopes to arrest the real killer in the very near future.

Laughing, I threw the paper onto the table, but then saw a small notice at the bottom of the page. I read it interestedly.

LOST

Mordecai Smith, boat man, and his son Jim left their house by the river at Millbank, London, in the steam launch *Aurora* at three o'clock last Tuesday morning. Since then there has been no news of them. Mrs Smith at Millbank (or at 221B Baker Street) will pay five pounds to anyone who can give her information about her husband and his launch.

'That notice is Holmes's idea,' I thought.

It was a very long day. I spent it waiting for a knock at the door with news of Mordecai Smith and the *Aurora*. I tried to read my book, but found it impossible not to think about Miss Morstan and the missing treasure.

At three o'clock I finally heard a knock at the door and Mrs Hudson brought Inspector Lestrade into the room.

'Is Mr Holmes out, sir?' he asked.

'He is,' I said. 'Please sit down, Inspector. Can I offer you a glass of **whisky**?'

'That's very kind, Dr Watson,' he said, sitting down in an armchair. 'Just a small one, with lots of water. It's a very hot day and this murder in Norwood is a real mystery.'

'So Mr Thaddeus isn't his brother's murderer, then?' I said, bringing Lestrade his drink.

'That's right,' Lestrade agreed. 'After he left Mr Bartholomew on the night of his death, he was with someone all the time. He can't be the murderer.'

The Inspector looked so disappointed I didn't like to **remind** him about Holmes saying Thaddeus Sholto was not his man.

'Your friend Mr Holmes is a wonderful man,' he said suddenly. 'He's clever and he never **gives up**. He's difficult sometimes, it's true, and he works in strange ways, but he's helped the police several times and I'm grateful to him for that.'

'What brings you here, Inspector?' I asked, smiling.

Lestrade took a paper from his pocket.

'I've received a telegram from Mr Holmes,' he replied.

I took the telegram from the Inspector and read it quickly.

whisky a strong alcoholic drink that is made in Scotland

remind to make somebody remember something

give up (*past* **gave, given**) to stop trying to do something

```
TO: INSPECTOR LESTRADE
SCOTLAND YARD

GO TO BAKER STREET IMMEDIATELY. IF I AM NOT THERE, WAIT
FOR ME WITH DR WATSON. WE HOPE TO FIND SHOLTO'S KILLER
TONIGHT.
HOLMES
```

'This is good news,' I said.

'Of course, it isn't **certain** that Mr Holmes will take us to the murderer,' said Lestrade, who had now finished his whisky.

His words made me angry, but before I could say anything, we heard someone coming up the stairs very slowly, breathing heavily. An old, white-haired sailor opened the door.

'Is Mr Sherlock Holmes here?' he asked in a dry voice.

'No,' I replied, 'but I work with Mr Holmes, so if you have a message for him you can give it to me.'

The old sailor stopped to think for a moment.

'I have to report my news to Mr Holmes himself,' he said.

'Is it about Mordecai Smith's launch? The *Aurora?*'

'Yes, I know where the men are and that treasure, too.'

'Then tell me,' I said, 'and I'll tell Sherlock Holmes when he returns.'

'No,' the man replied, 'I'll only talk to Mr Holmes himself.'

'Well, you must wait for him, then,' I said.

'I'm a busy man!' he answered. 'I can't wait for anyone.'

He turned to leave the room, but Lestrade had stood up and was now at the door.

'That's not possible, I'm afraid,' he said. 'You have important information and must stay here. Please sit down.'

'It's not fair,' said the old sailor, with an angry look on his face, but he sat down in an armchair.

Lestrade and I sat down at the table. I offered him a **cigar** and we continued our conversation. Suddenly we both heard Holmes's voice in the room with us.

certain sure

cigar a thick, brown cigarette

'Aren't you going to offer me a cigar too?'

We turned in surprise to see Holmes in the armchair where the old sailor had been sitting.

'Holmes!' I cried. 'But where's the sailor?'

'Here,' he said, and he pointed to a white **wig** on the table next to him. 'I'm your sailor! I'm very pleased you and the Inspector didn't recognize me! I've spent the day as an old man and a very interesting day, too. I understand Mr Thaddeus Sholto and his servants are no longer under arrest.'

Lestrade nodded sadly.

'Don't worry, Inspector,' Holmes went on. 'We'll soon have the real criminals. I need a fast police boat – a steam launch – at Westminster at seven o'clock this evening.'

Lestrade agreed immediately.

'I'll also need two strong police officers because there will be two or three men on the *Aurora*.'

Lestrade nodded.

'And finally, I'm sure that when we find the treasure, Dr Watson would like to take it to Miss Morstan, the owner.'

Lestrade looked a little worried for a moment.

'All right,' he said, 'but the police need to see it later.'

'Of course,' Holmes agreed. 'I think we'll have an interesting evening, gentlemen!'

Lestrade ate dinner with us. Holmes was now very bright and excited, while Lestrade seemed calmer. When Mrs Hudson had taken the plates away after our meal, Holmes gave a glass of whisky to Lestrade and another to me.

'A drink before we go,' he said. 'Watson, please bring your revolver with you. Our adventures tonight may be dangerous.'

He looked out of the window.

'Our cab's here,' he went on. 'Let's go.'

We reached Westminster just after seven o'clock. Our boat was waiting for us. Lestrade, Holmes and I boarded the launch and sat down at the back. There was a **crew** of two men and

wig false hair

crew the people who work on a boat

54

there were also two tall police officers on the boat.

'Where are we going?' asked Lestrade.

'To the **Tower** of London,' Holmes replied.

Our launch moved quickly away from the river bank.

'Good,' said Holmes. 'Our boat is a fast one. Watson, let me explain why we're here. The Baker Street boys couldn't find the *Aurora* anywhere on the river, but I knew the boat must be somewhere. Small and his associate were hiding, I was sure, until the time was right for them to leave the country. Suddenly I realized what they'd done: they'd left the *Aurora* with a boat builder and had probably asked him to do some small **repairs**. Dressed as an old sailor, I visited every boat builder on the river. I had no luck at the first fifteen builders, but at the sixteenth I found the *Aurora* and Mr Mordecai Smith himself! He was very drunk and was shouting at the boat builder, 'I want her tonight at eight o'clock and not a moment later! I have two gentlemen who won't wait!' Smith went back to the pub and I returned to Baker Street. We'll wait on the river for the *Aurora* to appear and when she does, we'll take Small, his associate and the treasure!'

'The plan might work, I suppose,' said Lestrade.

'We'll see, Inspector,' said Holmes, smiling.

tower a tall building

repairs things that are done to make something that is broken work again

READING CHECK

1 What do they say? Complete the sentences.

  1 'Are you all right?'

  2 ~~'I spent the night thinking about our problem.'~~

  3 'Perhaps you'd like a glass of whisky?'

  4 'Your friend Mr Holmes is a wonderful man.'

  5 'Is Mr Sherlock Holmes here?'

  6 'Do you have a revolver?'

  a Holmes says to Watson: .*'I spent the night thinking about our problem.'*

  b .... asks the sailor in a dry voice.

  c Holmes asks Watson ....

  d Watson asks Holmes ....

  e .... says Watson to Lestrade.

  f .... says Lestrade to Watson.

2 Put these sentences in order. Number them 1–6.

  a ☐ Watson goes to Camberwell to see Miss Morstan.

  b ☐ Inspector Lestrade arrives in Baker Street.

  c ☐ Holmes returns, dressed as an old sailor.

  d ☐ 1 ☐ Holmes and Watson wait in their rooms for Wiggins.

  e ☐ Holmes and Watson board a police launch with Lestrade.

  f ☐ Holmes goes down the river.

WORD WORK

1 Find words from Chapter 8 in the river.

crewrepairswhiskycigarwigtowerremindcertaingiveup

2 Use the words from Activity 1 to complete the sentences.

a My grandfather doesn't usually smoke, but occasionally he has a .cigar. after dinner.

b When she was ill she lost her hair, so she wore a .... over her bald head.

c When I call him, he never answers. I .... I won't phone him any more.

d We can't use our car at the moment. It's in the garage for ....

e He always forgets things. You have to .... him about everything.

f He drinks only Scottish .... He doesn't like the American or Irish kinds.

g There's no question. I'm .... I left the money here – and it's gone!

h From the top of the church .... you can see the whole town very well.

i The ship has a .... of three people and can take fifteen passengers.

GUESS WHAT

What happens in the next chapter? Tick two boxes.

a ☐ The police launch chases the *Aurora* down the river.

b ☐ Lestrade sees Thaddeus Sholto on the *Aurora*.

c ☐ Holmes and Watson shoot Jonathan Small's associate.

d ☐ The man with the wooden leg escapes.

e ☐ Lestrade arrests Mordecai Smith.

f ☐ Miss Morstan finally sees the treasure.

Chapter nine

Adventure on the River

The sun was going down when we reached the boat builder's place near the Tower of London.

'That's where the *Aurora*'s hidden,' said Holmes, pointing across the river. 'We'll wait here until we see her.'

We all watched carefully, and at eight o'clock, as Holmes had told us, the launch appeared. The *Aurora* was moving very quickly through the water.

'There she is!' cried Holmes. 'Let's go – as fast as we can!'

Our launch was soon travelling quickly down the river after the *Aurora*. The crew put more coal onto the fire to make her move as fast as possible. We **raced** past all kinds of boats and heard voices shouting at us as we passed. The *Aurora* went faster, and we followed her closely.

'We'll soon catch her,' said Lestrade.

But just then another launch suddenly moved across the river in front of us and we had to stop. When we started again, the *Aurora* was more than two hundred **yards** away. We were now far down the river. The sky was full of stars, so we could see the *Aurora* clearly in front of us. Lestrade turned our **searchlight** on her and we immediately saw the people on board. One man sat at the back of the launch with something that looked like a large dog at his feet. Next to him stood a boy. Mordecai Smith was busy throwing coal onto the fire as fast as he could.

The only thing we could hear now in the silence of the night was the sound of the *Aurora* as the launch moved quickly down the river.

'Stop!' shouted Lestrade.

We were very close, and both launches were travelling at top **speed**. At Lestrade's shout the man at the back of the *Aurora* stood up and shouted angrily back at us. He was tall

race to move very quickly

yard 0.9 metres

searchlight strong ship's light

speed how quickly something moves

and looked very strong, but I could see immediately that he had a wooden leg. As he stood up, I realized that the figure at his feet was not in fact a dog but a tiny dark-skinned man with an enormous head and long, dirty hair. He had the ugliest face that I've ever seen, and the look in his eyes was terrible. Holmes immediately took out his revolver, and I did the same.

'Shoot if he lifts his hand, Watson,' said my friend quietly.

We were only a few yards behind the *Aurora* now. Suddenly the black man pulled a short, round piece of wood from his pocket and put it to his lips. Holmes and I **fired** our revolvers at the same time and he fell back into the river. I saw his terrible eyes for a short moment before his head disappeared into the black water of the Thames.

Next the man with the wooden leg steered the launch to the river bank. We followed at top speed, but we were not quick enough to stop him jumping from the *Aurora*. Luckily for us, he didn't manage to move very far. At that place on the river the banks were very muddy and it wasn't long before the man's wooden leg was deep in the mud. He pulled and pulled, but he couldn't move. It was only with the help of a rope that we were able to pull him on board our launch. The man was **furious**, but there was nothing that he could do.

fire to shoot a gun
furious very angry

Lestrade ordered Mordecai Smith and the boy to board our launch and, although they looked very unhappy, they didn't try to escape. On the deck of the *Aurora* we could see a large Indian chest and we knew at once that it contained – or had contained – the Sholto family's treasure. There was no key, but Lestrade's men moved the heavy chest from the *Aurora* onto the police launch. It was terrible to think how many men had lost their lives for that treasure.

We tied the *Aurora* to the back of our launch and moved slowly back up the river. Lestrade shone the searchlight onto the water, but Small's **companion** had disappeared.

We sat opposite the man with the wooden leg. His skin was dark from the sun, and I could see that he'd spent much of his life outdoors. He looked more sad now than angry.

'Well, Jonathan Small,' said Holmes lighting a cigarette, 'can you tell us why you had to kill Mr Bartholomew Sholto?'

Small looked at us miserably.

'Tonga killed him,' he said, 'with one of his poisoned thorns. I was very angry with him, but it was too late. Sholto was already dead when I climbed through the window.'

Holmes offered him a cigarette and some whisky, which he accepted gratefully. The drink made him speak more freely.

companion
someone who
travels with you

'It was a terrible surprise,' he went on, 'seeing him dead with that awful smile on him. That wasn't part of my plan.'

At that moment Lestrade joined us.

'Mr Mordecai Smith tells me he didn't know anything about the Norwood murder.'

'It's true,' Small agreed. 'I paid him well, but I never told him anything about that.'

'Then we won't arrest him for the moment,' said Lestrade.

The launch stopped at Vauxhall Bridge for me to take the treasure to Miss Morstan as we'd agreed. Lestrade wanted to open the chest and examine it, but Small explained that he'd thrown the key into the Thames.

I travelled to Camberwell by cab with Sergeant Judd, who helped me to carry the chest to Miss Morstan's door. She was surprised to see me arrive so late in the evening, but she let me into the house immediately.

'I've brought you the treasure,' I said, with a heavy heart.

We sat down in the living room.

'Please tell me how you found it,' she replied.

She seemed interested, but not thrilled that the treasure chest was hers at last. I told her the story of our adventures, to which she listened very carefully.

'It's a beautiful chest,' she said when I had finished. 'Indian, I suppose. Where's the key?'

'In the Thames,' I answered. 'I'll have to break it open.'

It took some time, but we finally managed to open the chest. To our great surprise, it was empty!

'So the treasure is lost,' said Miss Morstan calmly.

I saw immediately that this fact did not **trouble** her.

'Thank God!' I cried.

She looked at me with a strange smile.

'Why do you say that?' she asked.

'Because I love you, Mary,' I replied, 'and now that there is no treasure between us, I can tell you.'

She looked into my eyes, and I knew then that we would be happy for ever.

trouble to worry; a worry or problem

READING CHECK

Are these sentences true or false? Tick the boxes.

		True	False
a	Holmes and Watson wait on the river for the *Aurora*.	☑	☐
b	The police launch follows the *Aurora* down the river.	☐	☐
c	With the searchlight Lestrade thinks that he can see a cat on the *Aurora*.	☐	☐
d	There are four people on board the *Aurora*.	☐	☐
e	Jonathan Small's associate shoots at the police launch with a revolver.	☐	☐
f	The police take a large Indian chest from the *Aurora*.	☐	☐
g	Lestrade offers Jonathan Small some whisky.	☐	☐
h	Miss Morstan is very sad that the treasure chest is empty.	☐	☐

WORD WORK

Match the words in the Indian chest with the correct definitions below.

a something that worries you ...*trouble*...

b to shoot a gun ....

c very angry ....

d to go very fast ....

e how fast something goes

....

f this person travels with you

....

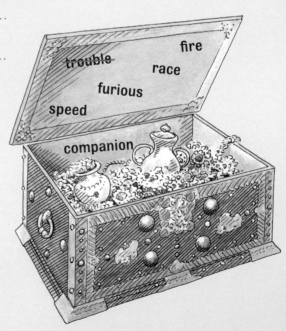

fire

trouble

race

furious

speed

companion

GUESS WHAT

What happens in the next chapter? Tick the boxes.

a Dr Watson and Sergeant Judd . . .

1 ☐ return to Baker Street.
2 ☐ go to Scotland Yard.
3 ☐ have dinner with Miss Morstan.

b Jonathan Small tells Lestrade . . .

1 ☐ where to find the treasure.
2 ☐ that the treasure is Major Sholto's.
3 ☐ that he will never find the treasure.

c Holmes invites Small . . .

1 ☐ to meet Miss Morstan.
2 ☐ to tell his story.
3 ☐ to visit him in Baker Street.

d Small says he lost his leg . . .

1 ☐ when he was attacked by natives.
2 ☐ when he was attacked by a crocodile.
3 ☐ in prison on the Andaman Islands.

e Watson tells Holmes . . .

1 ☐ that he is going back to Afghanistan.
2 ☐ that he is going to leave London.
3 ☐ that he is going to marry Miss Morstan.

The Sign of Four

I returned to Baker Street with Sergeant Judd. Holmes had just arrived with Lestrade and Jonathan Small because they had visited Scotland Yard on their way. I showed them the empty chest. Holmes laughed, but Lestrade was furious.

'What have you done with the treasure, Small?' he cried.

Jonathan Small stared back at him.

'I've hidden it in a place where you'll never find it,' he replied. 'That treasure belongs to me and three men who are still in prison in the Andaman Islands – The Sign of Four. That's why I threw it into the Thames – so that no one in the Sholto or Morstan family would have it! You'll find the treasure in the same place that you'll find little Tonga and the key.'

'Why didn't you throw the chest into the river? Why did you take the treasure out?' asked the Inspector.

Small looked very pleased with himself.

'Because I knew it would be much easier to find one chest at the bottom of the Thames than all the pieces of treasure in a hundred different places,' he replied.

'That was a very stupid thing to do, Small,' Lestrade told him. 'You haven't helped yourself.'

Small was now very angry.

'The treasure belongs to me and the others,' he repeated, 'not to any Sholto or Morstan. You have no idea of the price we paid to get that treasure, or the pain!'

'You're right,' Holmes said as he lit a cigarette. 'We haven't heard your story, so we don't know how you acquired the treasure. Please tell us.'

Small became a little calmer at Holmes's words.

'You've been fair to me, sir,' he said, 'so if you want to hear my story, I'll tell you. But there's a lot to tell. Perhaps I could have a drink?'

Lestrade nodded and Holmes gave Small a small glass of whisky. He took a drink and began his story:

I was born in the west of England, and my family were good, honest people. I always brought them a lot of trouble. When I was eighteen I joined the army and went to India. But I hadn't been there very long when I went swimming in the River Ganges. I was attacked by a **crocodile** and it bit my leg off. I almost died. I spent five months in hospital and when I came out, the army didn't want me any more. I was miserable for a while, but then a man called Abel White gave me work. It was a good job and I'd decided to spend the rest of my life working for him when suddenly the country was **at war**. One minute everything was calm, and the

crocodile this dangerous animal with short legs and a long tail lives in rivers and lakes in hot countries

at war when two countries are fighting

next minute two hundred thousand natives were attacking all the white men in India!

Night after night the sky was lit by burning houses on the hill tops. It was a terrible time. Every day we saw white men and their families on their way to Agra, where the nearest soldiers were. But Mr White refused to leave and I stayed with him – until the day that the natives came for him. They burned his house and murdered him. I found his body, half-eaten by wild dogs. Of course, I ran for my life.

Late one night I managed to reach Agra, but the **rebels** were everywhere. I joined the soldiers who were trying to **defend** the city, but it was impossible. Finally we had to hide in the old **fort** of Agra. It's an enormous place and we didn't have enough men to defend all the **gates**, so we had a group in the middle of the fort and one white man with two or three natives at each gate.

There were two **Sikhs** with me as their leader at one gate. We'd spent two nights together. They were both tall, strong men – Mahomet Singh and Abdullah Khan. They could speak English quite well, but they didn't say much. I stood alone at the gate, looking down on the river and the great city. We heard the rebels all night and could never forget the danger we were in.

The third night was dark and dirty, with heavy rain. At two o'clock in the morning I put down my gun to light a cigarette and immediately the Sikhs attacked me. They had knives, and I was too terrified to move.

'Don't make a noise,' said Khan.

'If you work with us tonight, you'll receive a quarter of some treasure that we're planning to steal. It will be divided between the four of us.'

'Who is the fourth person?' I asked.

'Dost Akbar,' he replied. 'Now, if you're with us, I will explain.'

I nodded to show that I agreed.

rebel a person who fights against the people who are in control

defend to fight to save something from attack

fort a strong building where soldiers live

gate a big door into a fort

Sikh a person from a religious group that began in the north of India

'There's a man in the north of the country who's very rich, although he doesn't have much land. When the trouble in the country started, he wanted to make sure that he wouldn't lose all his treasure, so he packed half of it in a chest and sent it here with one of his servants. This man is **disguised** as a **merchant** and he uses the name Achmet.

'He's now in the city of Agra, waiting to enter the fort. He has a companion: Dost Akbar, my **cousin**, who knows his secret. Dost Akbar will lead him to this gate tonight and when he arrives Mahomet Singh and I will kill him. The treasure will be ours. Now, will you help us?'

Here in London a man's life seems important, but in India at that time we saw death everywhere. I didn't know Achmet, but I could see immediately how the treasure would change my life. I agreed to help.

It was still raining and there were heavy brown clouds in the sky. Less than an hour after my conversation with Khan, Achmet arrived at the gate with Dost Akbar. Dost Akbar was an enormous Sikh with a long black beard, and Achmet was a small, fat frightened man.

'Please help us,' he said. 'We've travelled a long way and need a safe place to spend the night.'

disguised wearing something so that people cannot recognize you

merchant a person who buys and sells things

cousin the son (or daughter) of your father's (or mother's) brother (or sister)

I didn't want to speak to the man for long because I knew he was going to die.

'Enter,' I said. 'These men will show you the way.'

The two Sikhs took him away, but two minutes later Achmet came running towards me with Dost Akbar close behind. The Sikh was holding an enormous knife. I could see that the little merchant was going to escape, so I threw myself in front of him. He fell, and almost immediately he was dead. Dost Akbar had **plunged** the knife into his heart!

What we did that night was wrong, I know, but you must understand that I had no choice. I had to help them.

'Please continue,' said Holmes impatiently.

Small went on with his story.

We dug a hole, and buried the merchant. Then we opened the chest. There were **jewels** of every kind, hundreds of them, inside. They would be divided among the four of us. But for now we had to hide them.

We buried the treasure near the merchant's body, and I drew four maps and put the sign of the four of us on each one. We knew then that we would always be true to each other.

Well, I suppose that you gentlemen know what happened next. More British soldiers arrived in the country and drove the rebels back. Agra was taken by the British army and we were beginning to hope that we would be able to leave with our treasure. But then we were arrested for the murder of Achmet.

We were all found **guilty** and sent to prison for life, although nobody knew anything about the treasure. We were sent at first to prison in Madras, but later we were moved to the Andaman Islands. I was the only white prisoner there, so I didn't have a bad life. In the evenings I was even allowed to watch the army officers, Major Sholto and Captain Morstan, play cards with some

plunge to push a thing suddenly into something

jewel an expensive stone

guilty who has done something wrong

of the prison officers.

I noticed that the army officers always lost, and one night Major Sholto lost a lot of money. I heard him tell Captain Morstan that he was in serious **financial** trouble and would have to leave the army, and I saw my chance to escape.

I told the Major about the jewels and suggested that he and Captain Morstan should have **a fifth** of the treasure if they would help 'the four' escape. We agreed on a plan and I gave a map to Sholto and another to Morstan to show where the treasure was hidden.

You can probably guess the rest of the story. Sholto **tricked** us all and returned to England with the treasure. I was furious, but there was nothing that I could do until several years later when I saved the life of a native, Tonga, and he helped me to escape from the Andaman Islands. We came to England together and, if I'm not wrong, you know the rest, Mr Holmes.

We sat in silence for a long moment, then Lestrade spoke.

'Well, Mr Holmes, you've done well here,' he said, 'and now I must arrest you, Jonathan Small. Sergeant Judd is waiting downstairs with a cab.'

Small seemed strangely calm as he was taken away.

Holmes and I sat at the table and lit cigarettes.

'Holmes,' I said heavily, 'the adventure of the Agra treasure may be our last together.'

'Really?'

'I've asked Miss Morstan to marry me,' I went on, 'and I'm happy to say that she's accepted.'

'Yes,' Holmes replied calmly. 'I know.'

'Impossible!' I cried. 'We've told nobody.'

'Elementary,' said Holmes. 'Let me explain . . .'

financial to do with money

a fifth 20%

trick to make people believe something that is not true

READING CHECK

1 Put these sentences in the correct order. Number them 1–9.

a ☐ Abel White gives Small a job.

b ☐ Jonathan Small joins the army at eighteen and goes to India.

c ☐ Dost Akbar kills Achmet.

d ☐ Small is attacked by a crocodile in the Ganges and loses a leg.

e ☐ War breaks out in India and natives kill White.

f ☐ Small escapes to the fort at Agra but is attacked by two Sikhs.

g ☐ Small escapes from the Andaman Islands.

h ☐ Small and the Sikhs are arrested and sent to prison.

i ☐ Small and the Sikhs bury Achmet and the treasure.

2 Answer these questions about Jonathan Small's story.

a Who were the 'four'?

b Why were they sent to prison and how long for?

c Who were the army officers on the Andaman Islands?

d How did Major Sholto lose his money?

e What did Small give to Sholto and Morstan?

f Who took all the treasure?

g How did Small escape from the islands?

WORD WORK

1 Find eleven more words from Chapter 10 in the fort.

M	A	R	G	L	F	O	R	T	D
E	R	E	B	E	L	S	P	U	I
R	D	X	D	E	F	E	N	D	S
C	S	U	T	A	U	H	T	T	G
H	C	O	U	S	I	N	S	R	U
A	P	P	L	U	N	G	E	I	I
N	D	S	U	W	I	A	I	C	S
T	G	G	U	I	L	T	Y	K	E
F	E	S	J	E	W	E	L	S	D
F	I	N	A	N	C	I	A	L	S

2 Use the words from Activity 1 to complete the sentences.

a Jonathan Small hides in the old .fort. at Agra.

b Watson often does not recognize Holmes when he is ....

c The president has sent the army to fight against .... in the north of the country.

d The treasure chest was full of gold and ....

e Did you kill him? Are you .... of murder?

f I read the business pages of the newspaper for the .... news in them.

g You can't .... me! I know that what you're saying isn't true!

h My aunt and uncle have lots of children, so I have lots of ....

i I was so hot that I wanted to .... my head into some cold water.

j Through the metal ...., in the wall you could see the old sweet factory.

k Some people are ready to die to .... their country.

l Antonio, who makes his money buying and selling things, is a .... in Venice.

WHAT NEXT?

1 Have you seen any films of Sherlock Holmes stories? What were they like?

2 Which of these Sherlock Holmes stories would you like to read next? Why?

a **A Study In Scarlet:** The first Sherlock Holmes story, in which we meet the great detective and his companion, Dr Watson. For the first time Watson sees Holmes at work . . .

b **The Hound of the Baskervilles:** Holmes and Watson investigate strange deaths in the English countryside. People say they have seen or heard an enormous dog . . .

c **The Valley of Fear:** Sherlock Holmes receives a message from the famous criminal, Professor Moriarity, which warns him that a man will be murdered soon. But before the detective has time to do anything, he hears that the man in question has already been murdered . . .

Project A — *Writing a Newspaper Report*

1 Read the newspaper report. Answer the questions about it.

ARMY OFFICER DIES IN NORWOOD

Yesterday evening Major John Sholto died in bed at his home, Pondicherry Lodge, in Norwood, south London. He was 68 years old. His sons were with him when he died. Recently Major Sholto had fallen seriously ill. It is believed that he died because of his very poor health. He had lived in Pondicherry Lodge for the past five years. Years ago he worked as an officer in the British army in India and in the Andaman Islands. He leaves two twin sons behind him – Thaddeus and Bartolomew.

a Who died?

b When did he die?

c Where did he die?

d How old was he?

e Who was with him when he died?

f What had happened recently?

g Why did he die?

h How long had he lived at his present address?

i What happened years ago?

j Who does he leave behind him?

2 Use the information in the notes – and the report in 1 – to write a newspaper report about Bartholomew Sholto's death.

Murder in Norwood

Mr Bartholomew Sholto discovered dead by famous detective Sherlock Holmes

about midnight last night

in room at home, Pondicherry Lodge, Norwood, south London

32 years old

alone when died

recently discovered valuable Indian treasure in house

believed murdered in order to steal treasure

at present address since father died

years ago Major Sholto hid treasure in secret room in house

leaves one twin brother – Thaddeus

Murder in Norwood

3 Write notes to answer these questions about Tonga's death. Look back at chapter ten of *The Sign of Four* to help you.

a When did Tonga die?

b Where did he die?

c How did he die?

d Who was with him when he died?

e What had happened just before his death?

f What had happened some days before in Norwood?

g What had happened some years before on the Andaman islands?

h Who and what did Tonga leave behind on the *Aurora*?

4 Now write a newspaper report about Tonga's death.

Project B   *Island History*

1 Read about the history of the Andaman Islands and complete the timeline on page 75.

A short history of the Andaman Islands

People were living on the Andaman Islands – in the Bay of Bengal – over two thousand two hundred years ago. Some say that the first people lived there 30,000 to 60,000 years ago.

The name 'Andaman' was first used by Arab travellers in the 9th century. In 1290 Marco Polo wrote about the islands, but perhaps he only saw them from a ship. A British prison was built in the most important town – now Port Blair – in 1789, but many prisoners fell sick, and it closed after only seven years.

In 1839 Dr Helfer, a German visitor working for the Indian government, was killed by the natives of the islands. In 1858 – after the first Indian War of Independence – a second British prison was built on the island. In 1872, an island prisoner murdered Lord Mayo, who was the leader of the British in India at the time.

In 1896 the British started building a new prison – the Cellular Jail – on the islands. It was finished in 1902. Many Indian freedom fighters were held prisoner and died there.

The Japanese army attacked the islands in 1942 and stayed until 1945. After that the islands were British again for a time until they became part of newly independent India in 1947.

In 2001 the population of the Andamans was about 315,000. On 26th December 2004 a 10 metre high Tsunami hit the Andaman islands and it is believed that 7,000 people were killed.

Timeline of the Andaman Islands' History

200 BC	
	The name 'Andaman' was first used by Arab travellers.
1290	
	A prison was built by the British in Port Blair.
1796	
	Dr Helfer, a German visitor, was killed.
1858	
	Lord Mayo was murdered by an island prisoner.
1896	
	The Cellular Jail was finished.
1942	
	The Japanese army left the islands.
1947	
	The island population was about 315,000
2004	

2 Use these timeline notes to write a short history of Devil's Island.

1852 prison opened on Devil's island – in Caribbean near French Guiana – by French Emperor Napoleon III.

1852-1938 – over 80,000 French prisoners sent to island. Many never seen again – died of terrible illnesses. Few escaped – only ways out: jungle or boat.

1854 new law – freed Devil's Island prisoners stay on in French Guiana for same time again as in prison – or life if there over eight years.

1885 new law – criminals guilty of number of smaller crimes sent to island too. A few women also sent to French Guiana – idea to marry men after prison.

1895 French army captain Alfred Dreyfus sent to Devil's Island on January 5 as enemy of France – innocent.

1907 Plan to send women to French Guiana stopped.

1938 French government stopped sending prisoners to Devil's Island

1952 prison closed. Most prisoners to France – some stayed in French Guiana.

3 **Find out about the past of one of these islands, or about an island that interests you. Make a timeline and write a short history of your island.**

Robben Island, Cape Town, South Africa

Tasmania

Floreana, The Galapagos

GRAMMAR CHECK

Adjectives with –ed or –ing

We use adjectives ending in –ed to describe our feelings about something.

Major Sholto was worried when he received a letter from India.

Major Sholto was terrified by a face at the window.

We use adjectives ending in –ing to describe what something is like.

The letter from India was worrying.

There was a terrifying face at the window.

1 Choose the correct adjective to complete the sentences.

a Thaddeus was **surprised**/**surprising** that the man at his brother's house didn't know that he was coming.

b Mrs Bernstone was **pleased/pleasing** to see Thaddeus because she felt **worried/worrying** about his brother Bartholomew.

c The smile on Bartholomew's face was strange and **frightened/frightening**.

d Thaddeus looked **terrified/terrifying** when he realized that the treasure was missing.

e Holmes found some **interested/interesting** footprints on the floor of the room under the roof.

f When they got back to Baker Street the next morning, Holmes and Watson were **exhausted/exhausting**. It had been a long and **tired/tiring** night.

g Holmes was **disappointed/disappointing** not to be able to hire Mr Smith's boat.

h Watson didn't want Miss Morstan to think that he was **interested/interesting** in her because she was a rich woman.

i Miss Morstan didn't find the idea of being rich very **thrilled/thrilling**. She was more **worried/worrying** about Mr Thaddeus than the treasure.

j Sherlock Holmes never feels **tired/tiring** when he's working; having nothing to do is more **exhausted/exhausting** for him.

k Inspector Lestrade was **surprised/surprising** that Holmes knew so much information about what had happened.

GRAMMAR CHECK

Question tags

We can use question tags to check information, or to ask someone to agree with us.

There can't be another explanation, can there?

Captain Morstan and Major Sholto were close friends, weren't they?

The tag contains a subject + main verb or auxiliary verb to match the sentence.

Holmes hasn't solved the mystery already, has he?

When the sentence is affirmative, the tag is negative.

Miss Morstan received a valuable present, didn't she?

When the sentence is negative, the tag is affirmative.

You haven't got any of you father's letters, have you?

2 Complete the dialogue. Use question tags.

Watson: So have you solved the mystery yet?

Holmes: Not yet, but I'm beginning to understand. Miss Morstan received a valuable present, a) ..didn't she.. ?

Watson: That's right, Holmes.

Holmes: I discovered that it was a few days after the death of Major Sholto. The Major was Captain Morstan's only friend, b) ....?

Watson: Yes, but the Major didn't meet Morstan in England, c) ....?

Holmes: That's what the Major said, but Captain Morstan disappeared very suddenly, d) ....?

Watson: And Miss Morstan hasn't heard from her father for six years. He can't possibly be alive, e) ....?

Holmes: True. But maybe the Major was lying, and his heir wants to help Miss Morstan.

Watson: Miss Morstan is a very fine woman, f) ....?

Holmes: I'm not sure about that, Watson. I'll bring my revolver tonight.

Watson: It isn't going to be a dangerous night, g) ....?

GRAMMAR CHECK

Modal auxiliary verbs: must and can't for deduction

We can use must + infinitive without *to* to talk about things that we believe are very probable.

Miss Morstan's pearls are big and beautiful; they must be expensive. (= 99% sure)

We can use can't + infinitive without *to* talk about things that we believe are not possible.

Miss Morstan hasn't heard from her father for six years, so he can't be alive.
(= 99% sure he isn't)

3 **Choose the correct word and complete the sentences with the words in the box.**

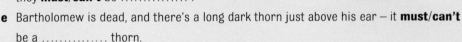

child	father's death	murderer	poisoned	screaming
tar	treasure	twins	wooden leg	wrong

a It **must/can't** be easy for Miss Morstan to hear about her .**father's death** .

b Bartholomew thinks that the .... **must/ can't** be worth half a million pounds.

c When we heard Mrs Bernstone ...., we knew that there **must/can't** be something wrong.

d Bartholomew's face is the same as Thaddeus's face; they **must/can't** be ....

e Bartholomew is dead, and there's a long dark thorn just above his ear – it **must/can't** be a .... thorn.

f There's a footprint and a round mark; it **must/can't** be the man with a .... But it's impossible to climb over the wall without help, so the man **must/can't** be alone.

g There are some little footprints in the small room under the roof, but Holmes thinks that the murderer **must/can't** be a .... The small footprints smell of .... so we **must/can't** be able to follow them.

h Inspector Lestrade thinks that Thaddeus **must/can't** be the murderer, but Holmes knows that Lestrade is ....

i Later, Lestrade finds out that Thaddeus was with someone all the time when Bartholomew died, so he **must/can't** be the ....

Reported speech with say, and reported commands with tell

In direct speech, we give the words that people say.	In reported speech, we put the verb one step into the past and change the pronouns and possessive adjectives.
'Our visitor has trodden in the tar,' he said.	*He said (that) their visitor had trodden in the tar.*

We can use *that* to introduce a reported statement, but it is not necessary.

We use tell + to + infinitive to report commands.

'Look at these footprints, Watson,' said Holmes.

Watson told Holmes to look at the footprints.

4 **Write the sentences again. Use reported speech.**

  a 'I know a dog that will be able to follow the smell of tar,' said Holmes.

  <u>Holmes said that he knew a dog that would be able to follow the smell of tar.</u>

  b 'There is a dead body and some valuable treasure has disappeared,' said Lestrade.

  ....

  c 'You have to take Miss Morstan home, Watson,' said Holmes.

  ....

  d 'If you don't go away, my dogs will attack you,' Sherman said to Watson.

  ....

  e 'I found a bag of thorns. The murderer dropped it when he left,' said Holmes.

  ....

  f 'Sholto lived happily in Norwood until a letter arrived from India,' Holmes said.

  ....

  g 'Small didn't kill Bartholomew, but his associate is a dangerous man,' said Holmes.

  ....

  ....

GRAMMAR CHECK

Past Simple, Past Continuous, and Past Perfect

We use the Past Simple to talk about things that happened at a specific time in the past and that are now finished.

Holmes visited every boat builder on the river.

We also use the Past Simple if two actions happen at the same time.

Smith went back to the pub and I returned to Baker Street.

We use the Past Continuous to talk about longer actions in the past.

Small and his associate were hiding.

We use the Past Perfect for actions that happened before other things in the past.

Suddenly I realized what they had done.

5 **Complete the text. Use the correct form of the verbs in brackets. Note that sometimes more than one tense is possible.**

Holmes, Watson, and Lestrade a) ..boarded.. (board) the police launch at seven o'clock. Holmes b) .... (find) the *Aurora* at a boat builder's near the Tower of London, and now they c) .... (wait) for the boat to appear. At eight o'clock Holmes d) .... (see) the *Aurora* and soon the police launch e) .... (travel) quickly down the river. Lestrade f) .... (turn) on the searchlight so they g) .... (can) see the people on the *Aurora*. Holmes h) .... (watch) the dark-skinned man carefully. Holmes and Watson i) .... (fire) their revolvers and the black man j) .... (fall) into the river. Small k) .... (steer) the *Aurora* into the river bank and quickly l) .... (jump) off. But Small m) .... (not manage) to move very far because his wooden leg n) .... (be) deep in the mud. With a rope they o) .... (pull) Small onto the police launch. Holmes p) .... (sit) opposite Small.

'Why q) .... (you, kill) Bartholomew Sholto?' Holmes r) .... (ask) him.

'I s) .... (not kill) him. Tonga t) .... (kill) him before I u) .... (can) stop him,' Small v) .... (explain).

Too and enough/not enough

We use too + adjective to say that something is more than necessary. We can add to + infinitive after the adjective to give more information about what we can or can't do as a result.

Small was too furious with Inspector Lestrade to tell his story.

We use adjective + enough to say that something is as much as necessary. We can add to + infinitive after *enough* to give more information about what we can or can't do as a result.

Small was clever enough to throw the treasure into the river.

We use not + adjective + enough to say that something is not as much as necessary.

At first, Small was not calm enough to tell his story.

6 Write the sentences. Use *too, enough*, or *not enough* with the adjectives in bold.

a After the crocodile attack, Small was **ill** and he couldn't stay in the army.

After the crocodile attack, Small was too ill to stay in the army.

b Abel White was **kind** and he gave Small a job.

....

....

c When the war started, it was **dangerous** and they couldn't stay at Mr White's house.

....

d The old fort at Agra was **big** and they couldn't defend all the gates.

....

e When the Sikhs attacked with knives, Small was **terrified** and he couldn't move.

....

f Small wasn't **strong** and he couldn't disagree with the Sikhs.

....

g Achmet wasn't **fast** and he couldn't escape from Dost Akbar's knife.

....

h Small was **slow** and he couldn't stop Tonga from killing Bartholomew Sholto.

....

GRAMMAR CHECK

Linkers: although, but, because, and so

Linkers are words that join two sentences together to make one. We use *although* and *but* to link two parts of a sentence with different ideas. We usually put although at the beginning of a sentence and but in the middle of a sentence.

Although Miss Morstan was calm, it was clear that she didn't want to waste time.

Miss Morstan was calm, but it was clear that she didn't want to waste time.

We use because to show the reason for something.

She put an advertisement in the newspapers because there was no news of her father.

We use so to show the result of something.

There was no news of her father, so she put an advertisement in the newspapers.

7 Complete the sentences. Use the words in the box.

so	although	but	so	although
but	because	so	because	

a Small wanted to leave prison, ...*so*... he told Major Sholto about the treasure.

b .... Major Sholto didn't kill Morstan, he knew that it was wrong to keep the treasure for himself.

c Small wanted to punish Major Sholto, ... it wasn't part of his plan to kill him.

d The doors and windows were locked, ... Small came into Bartholomew's room through a door in the roof.

e Tonga trod in some tar, ... Holmes could follow him with Toby.

f .... Mrs Smith didn't see Small, she heard his wooden leg as he walked away.

g At first, Holmes decided not to look for the *Aurora* .... there were too many places to hide the boat along the river.

h The Baker Street boys couldn't find the *Aurora* on the river .... Small had left the boat with a boat builder.

i Small jumped off the *Aurora*, ... his wooden leg was soon deep in the mud of the river bank.

DOMINOES Your Choice

Read *Dominoes* for pleasure, or to develop language skills. It's your choice.

Each *Domino* reader includes:
- a good story to enjoy
- integrated activities to develop reading skills and increase vocabulary
- task-based projects – perfect for CEFR portfolios
- contextualized grammar activities

Each *Domino* pack contains a reader, and an excitingly dramatized audio recording of the story

If you liked this *Domino*, read these:

The Faithful Ghost and Other Tall Tales

Selected by Bill Bowler

A 'Tall Tale' is a story that's hard to believe, and the five tall tales in this book all tell of ghosts. Some have dark secrets buried in the past, others bring messages for the living. Some are laughable, some are sad, and some are just evil.

Sometimes there's a logical explanation for the strangest happenings, but often things cannot be explained by logic alone. Either way, you're sure to find some frightening reading between the covers of this book.

Hard Times

Charles Dickens

Thomas Gradgrind believes that facts and money are more important than feelings and imagination. After Sissy Jupe – a circus child – is left alone in the world, Gradgrind takes her into his house, looking after her and teaching her facts with his own children Tom and Louisa. Some years later the Gradgrind family meets hard times. Louisa becomes a prisoner in a loveless marriage, and Tom has problems at work.

In the end, Thomas Gradgrind learns the importance of feelings and imagination.

	CEFR	Cambridge Exams	IELTS	TOEFL iBT	TOEIC
Level 3	B1	PET	4.0	57-86	550
Level 2	A2–B1	KET-PET	3.0-4.0	–	390
Level 1	A1–A2	YLE Flyers/KET	3.0	–	225
Starter & Quick Starter	A1	YLE Movers	1.0–2.0	–	–

You can find details and a full list of books and teachers' resources on our website:
www.oup.com/elt/gradedreaders